TOO BUSY FOR YOUR OWN GOOD

Get More Done in Less Time— with Even More Energy

CONNIE MERRITT

New York Chicago San Francisco Lisbon London Madrid Mexico City
Milan New Delhi San Juan Seoul Singapore Sydney Toronto

Library of Congress Cataloging-in-Publication Data

Merritt, Connie.
  Too busy for your own good : get more done in less time — with even more
energy / Connie Merritt.
      p.   cm.
  Includes index.
  ISBN 978-0-07-161286-9 (alk. paper)
  1. Time Management.   I. Title.

BF637.T5.M47   2009
640'.43—dc22   2008054055

1 2 3 4 5 6 7 8 9 10 11 12 13 14 15 16 17 18 19 20 21 22   FGR/FGR   0 9

ISBN 978-0-07-161286-9
MHID   0-07-161286-6

Interior design by Sue Hartman
Interior artwork by James Silvani

McGraw-Hill books are available at special quantity discounts to use as premiums and
sales promotions or for use in corporate training programs. To contact a representative,
please visit the Contact Us pages at www.mhprofessional.com.

This book is printed on acid-free paper.

This book is dedicated to all of you

who are too busy and want more out of your life—

you know who you are.

Contents

Part 1 # The New Culture
of Busyness

Part 2 Work Is Great,
Except I'm So Busy

Part 3 # Dealing with Busyness at Home

Acknowledgments

At the many turning points of my life there were guides who gave me hope, support, and love. To recognize all of them would take another book but, like an eagerly anticipated child being born, this book has many special godparents. A big thank-you goes to John Aherne, Joe Berkowitz, and their colleagues at McGraw-Hill for encouraging me to write this, along with their wise and thoughtful guidance in clarifying my voice on paper.

Foremost, I want to thank my husband, Lynn Hughes, for keeping me and the critters safe and warm all these years: you're my rock, my love, my life. To Nancy Brundage, whose constant friendship all these years (decades!) I value: I admire your sensibility and strength. To Lola Gillebaard, whom I admire because she lives life not only heroically but also hilariously: I'm grateful for your love and friendship. To Luke Yankee, whose friendship I treasure not only for its loyalty: you help me dream the impossible and believe in its manifestation.

To all those in my minichurch group, my appreciation abounds for your love, spiritual support, and constant prayers: Jim Aten, Valerie and Bill Garrett, Susan Lindstrom, Helen and Geoff Gilchrist, Lola and Hank Gillebaard, Linda and Jim Loomis, Gretchen and Dick Miller, and Glyn and

Jeanna Riley. Lots of pats and love go to my barn buddies: Janice Posnikoff, D.V.M.; Marcy Bisson; Victoria Rea; and Dana Butler-Moberg and her staff and volunteers at the Shea Therapeutic Riding Center. For support in lots of ways, I thank June Stockdale, Liz Yapp, and Beverly St. Clair. I am so blessed!

Introduction

The trouble with being in the rat race is that even if you win, you're still a rat.

—Lily Tomlin

While standing in line for a cup of coffee recently, I witnessed a reunion between two women who obviously knew each other well. After their initial greetings, they proceeded to try to top each other as to who was the busiest. One had a job with lots of overtime under the threat of unemployment, along with a family to feed and clothe and a house to keep tidy and maintained. The other had one of those "gifted" preschoolers who required every kind of over-the-top activity and special tutoring to get into Harvard. I found myself thinking, "Pffffft, try working my schedule, then you'd know what busy really is." Then I realized that, just like these women, I had fallen into the "competition for busyness" trap. Since when did busy become the latest status symbol?

Our society seems to have changed more in the past thirty years than it did in the entire previous millennium; we've become wired, not just in the digital sense, but wired in the activity sense. In our efforts to have it all, we've created a culture of busyness. But is it working? Do we lead balanced lives with a sense of purpose, or do we just have a to-do list that we'll never get completed?

An Early Start to Busy

I've always been in a hurry. I was born in less than an hour and premature to boot. By age twelve, I knew by heart the formula for my father's foamless detergent manufacturing process, and I balanced the company books. I never walked anywhere in high school—I ran or did a cross between the military march and modern dance to get where I was going. I completed my five-year college program in four years. The only thing that mattered to me was what was next.

When I got my first computer in the mid-eighties, I was thrilled at how much time it saved me writing letters, keeping track of people, and organizing my finances. Then I got a fax machine. Whoopee, I didn't have to wait on the postal service to get things done quickly. Then came the Internet, cable, cell phones, PDAs, and a caffeine-delivery system on every corner. Earth had become heaven, custom-made for a zoom freak like me.

My "busy" started to become *too* busy almost imperceptibly, and soon all the time-saving technology convinced me to use my extra time to do extra work. Gradually I became a slave to the speed at which newer technology and new gadgets allowed me to work. I was living the multitasker's dream—more speed, more work, more stimuli, more responses required. Faster! Better! More!

I became a poster child and champion of the overbooked, overcommitted, and overstressed control freak. This became strikingly clear the morning I woke up with a massive pressure in my chest and the inability to catch my breath. The more I tried to calm myself down, the worse my symptoms got. I had a fleeting thought that I should probably see a doctor, but how could I find the time?

Emergency Wake-Up Call

My husband kept asking, "What's wrong? Should I call 911?" As a former trauma nurse, I went through the checklist. Shortness of breath? Chest pain? Left arm numbness? Indigestion? Light-headedness? Yes, yes, yes, yes.

Egads, I was diagnosing my own heart attack! My thought right before I passed out was, "This can't be happening to me—I'm barely fifty!"

When I woke up, four burly firemen in my bedroom were strapping me to a gurney. Ever the control freak, I was barking orders at them even as they negotiated our stairwell: "Watch the handrail! Easy on the new paint! Tip me this way."

As one rookie paramedic attempted to start an IV line in my arm, I pointed to my left arm and said, "No, not that vein, it was blown years ago. Use this one." As they attached me to the heart monitor, I twisted around, practically upside down, to check the EKG tracing.

"Normal sinus rhythm, run another lead!" I barked between shrieks of pain.

We finally arrived at the emergency room, after what was probably the most irritating ambulance ride of the attendants' careers. This was the same ER I'd worked in years ago, before I became a full-time professional speaker and road warrior.

Thanks to the wonders of modern pharmacology, the staff was finally able to calm me down, and they ran several tests. After a few hours, the doctor came in with *that* look on his face. You know, the look that says, "I need to deliver bad news, and I'm not looking forward to it."

He leaned against the end of my bed and said, "I believe you have had a massive . . . panic attack."

What? This diagnosis just did not seem possible. I was in total control of my life. I couldn't possibly be having a panic attack. Or so I thought.

Before being discharged, I was given strong warnings to slow down, eat better, and get some rest. It was suggested that I follow up with my doctor to find a professional trained in stress reduction. My fellow nurses were also kind enough to remind me that, as a former nurse myself, I'd once cared for many of those who didn't heed these kinds of warnings. They jogged my memory of treating victims of terrible accidents caused by driving while drowsy, young executives having dreadful heart attacks, and witnessing other patients' psychiatric stays for emotional collapse.

Ultra-Busy Control-Freak Rehab

Before you go thinking that I miraculously converted myself from the ultra-busy control freak into the countess of calm, let me assure you that old habits do indeed die hard. Just because I was scared witless during my trip to the ER and was nagged by my family, friends, and physicians to *slow down* doesn't mean I actually wanted to get off my crazy but familiar treadmill.

I was secretly sad that I didn't have a heart attack. From all my cardiac nursing experience, I *knew* how to rehabilitate a heart attack, but I didn't have a *clue* as to how to recover from a panic attack. But in true ultra-busy control-freak fashion, I set out to fix the problem. I got myself into therapy, found a cause that I loved, and after much thought and the advice of my physician, decided to try some medication to help with my stress levels.

At the onset of my panic attack rehab program, I had a secret, burning hunger to recapture the passion for life that I'd had when I was younger. You know, that "I'm going to save the world" passion and energy. This was beyond midlife crisis and the longing for lost youth. I was looking for meaning and purpose, something beyond myself. I wasn't looking to wind down or retire, but for a vision and a point of focus for the next (and perhaps final) act of my life.

I took a hard, critical inventory of how I spent my time, what my goals were, and what I wanted my life to look (and feel) like. I took a magnifying lens to my health, home, community, relationships, career, money, personal development, and spirituality.

Making the changes I needed to be a recovering ultra-busy control freak have been challenging and, at times, all-consuming. But I believe I have saved my sanity, my marriage, and, perhaps, my life.

Surf Lessons

My grandmother wouldn't tolerate me complaining or not taking responsibility for my own life. I can recall having lunch on her beautiful seaside patio years before my panic attack. I was bemoaning the economy, unsatisfactory relationships, and my disappointments. She looked at me and said, "Connie, stop yelling at the waves and just learn how to surf." She was a major fan of the phrase "just do it" before a certain shoe company even had a clue. Only when you accept that it's your responsibility—your job—to overcome busyness will you be able to do so.

This book brings together the stories and advice I've received from countless interviews with men and women who are deep in the trenches of busy, modern lives. I've also included pearls of wisdom from leaders in the fields of business, medicine, and mind-body research. Reading these pages and doing the exercises is a way for you to pump the brakes on your busyness and start living with clarity instead of craziness, harmony instead of hostility, and satisfaction instead of sorrow. In other words, get ready to learn how to surf!

Part 1

The New Culture of Busyness

Chapter 1

Are You in over Your Head?

Beware the barrenness of a busy life.

—Socrates

When you discovered that you could not only bring home the bacon but fry it in a pan while feeding the baby at the same time, you probably got a certain high just from getting all of it done. Then you found you could add a call to your best friend. And start a load of laundry. And floss your teeth. Then you may have asked yourself whether you could also outline your sales presentation. The answer: "Yes . . . I . . . *can!*"

Once you start asking yourself what else you can manage to fit in, where does it end? If you're not careful, you'll get sucked deeper and deeper into your "activity abyss." Pretty soon you'll have lost the basic ability to be present, not to mention your fundamental joy in life. And that's no way to live. But unfortunately these days it seems all too common.

Busyness Is the New Status Symbol

As a society we are obsessed with being busy. We seem to actually pride ourselves on getting as little sleep as possible and being overworked because we're looking for *satisfaction* and *significance*. For modern women and men, *busy* has become the newest status symbol. We are at risk for burnout or—even worse—rust-out! We are experiencing not just physical signs of stress, such as insomnia, indigestion, and headaches, but also unrealized dreams, along with empty nests, raging hormones, and aging parents. Modern life is not for wimps.

If everyone else is busy, then what's the big deal? Your friends and coworkers seem to madly dash around to get their to-dos done. Admit it, if someone tells you how busy they are, you feel the urge to tell them that you're *much* busier. In fact, you're so busy you haven't slept a consecutive eight hours since the late nineties. If you offer enough proof to get your competitor to concede the point, then congratulations. You win! But what have you got to show for it?

Busyness has been called a "soft addiction." When you're moving fast and getting things done, you get a little psychic—and physical—boost. It's as though your energy produces even more energy—a sort of high, not unlike that of a drug addict. As with most addictive behaviors, that feeling doesn't last for very long, and then you need even more to get that high again. Is your striving for *more* making you more busy than you can handle?

What if you're a frazzled, single working mom struggling to keep your head above water? Striving or struggling, you've probably gotten busier than you could handle without even realizing how bad it was getting. Like water slowly dripping onto a stone, every bit of busyness has the power to slowly and imperceptibly wear you down. It's as though you're a circus juggler starting with two balls. You get really good with two, so you add another. Then you get good with three and add another, and so on. Pretty soon you're juggling chainsaws, wondering, how did *this* happen?

One of my students told me that she was good at tuning out all distractions so she could really focus on a project and meet her deadline. Recently, though, she was feeling bothered and unfocused at work. "When I landed this job, I was bothered by the phones ringing, colleagues chatting, even the noise from street traffic, but I learned to tune it out. Now, I snap at people, and I'm always running late. I'm smart. I'm capable. Why can't I get my job done?"

Demanding constant high-intensity output is hard on your body, heart, and soul, frequently leading to a fraying of your nerves and dwindling of your energy. You need breaks, balance, and breathing space. Be careful when you relentlessly keep yourself focused, productive, busy—*on*. The body takes what it needs, whether you've scheduled it or not.

Are You Too Busy for Your Own Good?

Busyness is personal. What you call normal might be considered overly busy and stressful to the next person. Although it's hard to quantify exactly how busy you are, this quiz will guide you in determining if it's affecting your life adversely.

Go through the following list and check all of the statements that are true for you:

☐ Are you working hard but feeling like you're not getting enough done?

☐ Do you feel underappreciated for your work or all you do at home?

☐ Do you multitask in the car, while exercising, or at meals?

☐ Do you have difficulty falling or staying asleep?

☐ Do you ever skip meals or find yourself eating too fast?

☐ Do you often lose or misplace important items or documents at home or work?

☐ Have you ever missed family members' events because of work?

☐   Are you mentally scattered or not feeling in control?

☐   Are you more sad, grumpy, short-tempered, or angry with people in the past six months?

☐   Do you refuse sex or intimacy because you're too tired?

☐   Do you use caffeine, energy drinks, or over-the-counter stimulants to push past your fatigue more than once a week?

☐   Do you feel alone and unsupported when facing emotional or physical problems?

☐   Do you often splurge or overspend to treat yourself after a big week?

☐   Do you tell at least one person how busy you are every day?

☐   Do you get frequent headaches, indigestion, fatigue, or body aches and pain?

☐   Are your shoulders and neck tight right now?

☐   Have you skipped or forgotten appointments in the past six months?

☐   Do you skip exercise because you're too tired?

☐   Do you beg off meeting with friends because of your workload or being tired?

☐   Have you skipped downtime, hobbies, or spiritual activities, such as church, meditation, yoga, or praying in the past week?

☐   Are you always available to take calls from work?

Total number of statements checked: _____

Scoring Your Busyness Level

1–5 **You are busy** and starting to get frustrated, but with some attention to the problem and a little fine-tuning, you can turn it around.

6–10 **You are too busy** and starting to show cracks in your physical health, mental well-being, and relationships. Make a commitment to take better care of yourself.

11–15 **You are ultra-busy,** exhausted, and facing burnout. Your health is being compromised, and your relationships are in jeopardy. Make a plan and start working it to save your body, mind, and soul.

16–21 **You are in the danger zone:** if you don't start making serious changes now, you are surely heading for serious health consequences and relationship breakdowns.

I Can't Get No Satisfaction, or How Does Your Wheel Roll?

How do you know whether you're ultra-busy? For one thing, you've probably been neglecting one of the key areas in your life. Sometimes it's hard to determine whether we're too busy overall because some areas in life are still running perfectly smoothly. However, when you're firing on all cylinders all the time, something's got to give. I want to give you a very simple and quick method for assessing your current level of satisfaction. You'll see that the way you allocate your busyness may have been sabotaging your satisfaction and quality of life.

Like so many of my coaching clients, one executive began our first session with, "Things are OK at work, my family's good, but I just feel like something's missing." I had her do the following exercise, and she quickly identified that the something missing was balance. Our plan for working together became to focus on certain areas of dissatisfaction and distribute her activities accordingly.

Take out a blank piece of paper and draw a large circle on it. Divide it into six equal parts—as if it were a wheel with six spokes or an apple pie sliced into six equal pieces.

Label each piece of the circle with one of the six major areas of your life:

▶ **Career:** your job, career opportunities, business involvement
▶ **Money:** the state of your finances, budget, insurance, investments
▶ **Health:** your physical condition, fitness, well-being, appearance

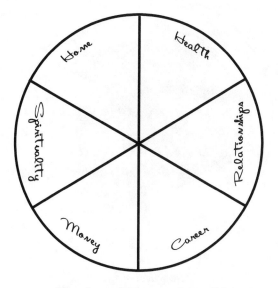

The six major areas of your life

▶ **Spirituality:** your practice of faith, matters of soul, self-development
▶ **Relationships:** interactions with your family, friends, coworkers, community
▶ **Home:** where you live, the condition and comfort of your environment

On a scale of one to ten (ten being the highest), rate your satisfaction in each of the six areas. With the center of the wheel being "zero" and the outer circle a "ten," shade in each area (or piece of the pie) with the corresponding number. Draw a line halfway between the center and the border of that pie piece and shade it from center to that line. For example, the illustration shows satisfaction in the money area as a 5. Continue with all six areas.

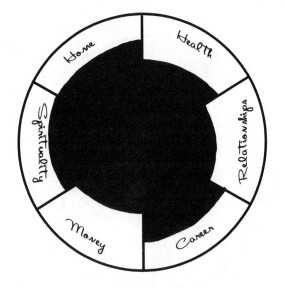

The wheel of life

Look at your wheel. This is an illustration of how your life is rolling along. If it were an actual wheel, would it roll smoothly with the spokes hitting the ground evenly? Or would it clunk and bump along like a flat tire on your car? When you're balanced, your life rolls along more smoothly, and satisfaction is the result.

If you're like most folks, the areas you rated the highest in satisfaction are the ones that you put the most time and energy into. Because you put the most time and energy into them, you get the most satisfaction or payback. Conversely, you probably avoid putting energy into those areas with which you aren't very satisfied.

If this sounds like a vicious cycle, it is. But the good news is that you can change all that—your busyness, your balance, and your happiness. You might think that you're busy because you have to be, or because you want to be. But why are you *really* busy? This book is aimed at helping you find the answer and giving you the tools to get your busyness in balance so you will have more satisfaction and meaning in your life.

De-Busify Now!

Some of the audience members at my workshops have told me that as long as they're still putting one foot in front of the other, they'll keep powering forward. In a way, this is true—I know how to ignore a twitching eye or back spasm and "carry on." Right before the personal collapse that landed me in the ER, I was doing call-in radio shows before the sun came up, speaking around the nation several times a month, writing books, and monitoring my grandmother's care in assisted living, all while being a newlywed, daughter, friend, and business owner. It felt normal to me, but my body let me know that it wasn't normal.

You might not be aware of how your own busyness and overstimulation have gotten out of hand. The type of busy that overtakes your life does so incrementally, not all at once. You've probably added tasks, behaviors, and thoughts little by little, so that you were never fully aware that your busyness level was going into the danger zone.

Don't be a casualty; de-busify now! Use the information in this book to de-stress and rebalance your life. Your body, soul, friends, and family will all be grateful that you did. Every great journey begins with one first step. Take a look at some of the reasons you're so busy. After reading the entire book, focus on the areas in which you're feeling the most frustrated, angry, out of control, or hopeless. Find the skills, tips, answers, and suggestions that work for you.

Happy de-busifying!

Chapter 2

What Are Your Reasons for Being Too Busy?

It is not enough to be busy. So are the ants. The question is, what are we busy about?

—Henry David Thoreau

What are the *real* reasons you fill your days and nights with activities until you've run yourself ragged? "Who else is going to do it?" "What choice do I have?" Yes, but why else? Go deeper. You are part of a culture of overachievers who aim to be deliriously happy and wildly successful at the same time rather than merely content and comfortable. But your reasons for being busy go beyond that. Perhaps you're proving your worth to an estranged family or showing the old neighborhood that you've succeeded in spite of your troubled teens. Possibly you just want to fit into a clique that you fought hard to be accepted by or thumb your nose at the bully who claims you'll never amount to anything.

In any case, it's important that you know your reasons for being so busy. Once you've pinpointed your reasons, it's easy to weigh them out and see whether they're really as valid as you think—they probably aren't. In this chapter, we'll also be taking a look at some of the excuses a lot of people make. Excuses are feeble, often unconscious attempts to explain why some behavior really isn't your fault. It usually involves placing blame on outside people or forces. The difference between reasons and excuses is accountability for your decisions and actions. You may even be unaware of how this difference affects your outlook and, ultimately, your life. But you can learn to recognize when you are making excuses and take control of your busyness. This just might mark the difference between a too-busy life and a life you love.

Why Are We So Busy?

The answer just might lie within the ever-increasing productivity of the U.S. workforce. According to the Bureau of Labor Statistics, the total number of hours worked weekly has remained essentially static for thirty years, but productivity has climbed steadily during the same period. As a nation, we're using technology to work harder and increase our output, not to help us slow down or ease our workloads.

Working away from the office is also a factor leading to being overly busy. Cell phones, e-mail, and telework all have helped to turn many homes into an office away from the office. When our BlackBerries are on constantly, we're so connected and hooked into work that our official office hours are extended to "indefinitely."

Also, lest we forget, work is not the sum total of our existence. Each of us has many different roles in life. On any given day you may be a worker, a partner, a parent, a spouse, a child, a leader, a friend, a consumer, and an audience desperately in need of entertainment for unwinding. Filling all of these roles is demanding. Each one requires that you maintain the same pace and productivity, but obviously that is not possible. Everything and everyone in your life is competing for a piece of you, just as you want your fair share. So you get busy and stay busy, even though there is only so much of you to go around.

The RQ Test (Find Out the "Reasons Quotient" of Your Busyness)

As I said before, in order to tame the ultra-busy lifestyle you've created, it is important to explore your reasons for it being that way in the first place. Investigating the deeper motivations behind your busyness allows you to loosen the grip that frenetic activity has on you. This self-discovery will empower and strengthen you to make positive changes in your behavior and, ultimately, your busyness.

For each statement that is true for you **frequently**, give yourself **3**.

For each statement that is true for you **sometimes**, give yourself **2**.

For each statement that is true for you **infrequently**, give yourself **1**.

For each statement that is **never** true for you, give yourself **0**.

1. When I have a list of things to do, I feel like I can't slow down or let up until I get them all done. _____

2. When people complain about their job or money, I think, "Just shut up, get busy, and things will be better." _____

3. My kind of job isn't that easy to come by, and I need to perform at a high level in order to keep it or move up in my profession. _____

4. My industry is 24/7/365 or has a strong international presence. I often telecommute and can be reached for work queries most anytime. _____

5. I need the money more than ever because the economy is such a mess. _____

6. My family depends on me to do all of this. _____

7. My personal digital assistant is left on during evenings, weekends, and personal time. _____

8. My parents weren't successful, and I don't want to be like them. _____

9. I don't have time to even think about a mate, let alone date. Love? Forget it, I'm too busy! _____

10. People seem to respect and treat me better when they know how busy I am. _____

11. The world is a mess. If we don't save it, who will? _____

    Total _____

Results

0–11   **Congratulations!** You are busy, but your natural immunity is fighting off an acute infection. Busyness isn't your permanent style, just a temporary approach to life that you can tame easily.

12–21 **You've got the busyness disease.** You're listening a little too much to the world and not enough to your own healthy thoughts and plans. Decide to be busy for significance, not success in the worldly sense.

22–33 **You've got the busyness plague,** and it's not looking good at the moment. Your busyness is stressing you to the point that soon you'll be unhealthy, bitter, and cynical. You could be so much happier, but you must focus your attention and work with diligence to turn this around.

How Valid Are Your Reasons?

Without letting personal responsibility off the hook, I believe there are some very powerful forces working on us—childhood, our parents, education, jobs, and a million other circumstances on this planet we call home. These forces have a gradual and cumulative effect, developing slowly but surely and becoming well established before becoming apparent. Being too busy sneaks up on you, and before you know it, you're ultra-busy. Let's explore those forces and your top offenders. For those statements in the RQ Test you felt were true for you "frequently" or "sometimes," read the following responses to examine the possible reasons for your busyness.

The Tasks Master

"When I have a list of things to do, I feel like I can't slow down or let up until I get them all done." You have replaced quantity for meaning in your day-to-day tasks. You think getting it all done is the goal. Sure, advertising and the media tell you to live life to the hilt and that you're going to miss out on something if you aren't constantly doing more, faster and better than anyone else. There is also a danger that by doing everything this way, you will race through your pleasurable activities too. Learn to say no and be careful why, how, and when you add to your list of things to do.

Time Is of the Essence

"When people complain about their job or money, I think, 'Just shut up, get busy, and things will be better.' " You treat time as a commodity. Your mind-set is that if you waste time, you are losing opportunities. This is not necessarily everyone's experience. Even though you may always try to do things

that you consider "worthwhile" so that you get a sense of accomplishment, be mindful that you are setting yourself up to be consumed by your busyness. Often you're feeling guilty that you can't fix others' problems for them, so you dismiss their concerns. When your goal becomes the movement, not the moment, you miss connecting with others and putting compassion into practice.

Married to Your Job

"My kind of job isn't that easy to come by, and I need to perform at a high level in order to keep it or move up in my profession." Dwindling job security isn't just in your particular industry; it's the norm today. Companies are always trying to reduce labor costs by outsourcing, moving, or merging jobs. People rarely feel secure, and there doesn't seem to be a time at work that you can say that you're content and protected from outside forces. The more skilled young people begin to enter the workforce, the more you feel pressure to work longer hours and be more productive just to protect your job. You need to keep pushing yourself to work smarter, not harder and longer. In Chapter 5, I will give you a bunch of ways to do just that!

You are also probably working too many hours. There used to be a time when employees showed up for work on Monday for the first of five eight-hour days in a row, had a two-day weekend, and started over again the following Monday. As reported by the Bureau of Labor Statistics, U.S. workers spent an average of 39.5 hours a week at work in 2007. This number is essentially the same as the 39.4-hour average in 1989 and the 40-hour week reported in 1967. In reality, today many jobs have mandatory overtime if you want to move up in the organization. If you frequently need to go the extra mile, be mindful of your physical health and make your home more of a sanctuary from work.

Work-Life Imbalance

"My industry is 24/7/365 or has a strong international presence. I often telecommute and can be reached for work queries most anytime." The boundaries between home and work are blurred. Advanced communication technology allows you to work from anywhere, and some managers expect you to be connected in your home, your car, and on vacation. You must carve out time slots and activities when you are not available and not checking your devices frequently and set your boundaries. There has to be time spent "off the grid" every single day.

You are living in a world that is always "on." Some places, such as police stations, fire stations, and hospitals, never close. It's up to you to work your hours and then leave your worries and concerns with the next shift. This involves confidence in your coworkers and strong interpersonal communication skills. If you work in an organization where your expertise may be needed at odd hours, train yourself to turn off your involvement as soon as your shift is over. No matter how urgent the problem seems, if it's during suppertime with your family, your colleagues at work will survive without you.

Money Problems

"I need the money more than ever because the economy is such a mess." You think money will solve your problems. Increasing your busyness just to make more money is not the answer—planning is. If you constantly tell yourself that you're going to lose your job and become a homeless person, you're putting yourself into a steady state of anxiety. When you have "money tunnel vision," you invest lots of mental and emotional energy in making money, leaving you unable to see the good in your life. World economics may be baffling,

and you can't directly control what our leaders are doing, but you can control your own world of money. Take a cold, hard look at your own finances, make a plan to cut spending, and clean up your credit.

Overcare

"My family depends on me to do all of this." You're experiencing overcare—the sense that you have to take care of everyone because no one else will. As head of the family, you take on responsibility for everyone, but they can always shoulder some of the burden too. Family roles have changed, as single parents tend to head up more households, adult children live at home longer, and elderly relatives need supervision. Sprawling suburbs full of dual-career families and retirement communities of elderly folks have exploded. As CEO of your family, it's time for you to restructure your home responsibilities and schedule so all members are doing their share. Everyone needs to pitch in. I will provide you with tips for getting this done in Chapter 10.

Technological Malfunction

"My personal digital assistant is left on during evenings, weekends, and personal time." You have stimulation overload. Technology is pushing you to move faster. Remember that *you* own your wired device, *it* doesn't own you. Being constantly connected makes you feel like you always have to be on the move or must be doing something. You get the feeling that if you don't work at or above the same pace that your latest lightening-fast chip does, you will fall behind. Set and stick to your own set of rules for when you have your devices on and when you check them. Later I will explain how to train yourself, your friends, and your family to give you some space.

Our Parents Cast a Long Shadow

"My parents weren't successful, and I don't want to be like them." The people who raised you have a significant influence on how you conduct your life. Volumes have been written on how deeply driven by and conflicted we are between wanting to please, rebel against, or emulate our parents. Many of us, at some time or another, experience very complicated relationships with them. Work on not being so hard on the folks who you think could have parented you better. Thanks to reality TV, the Internet, and the celebrity-hungry media, we have lots of celebrities but too few heroes. The bar has been lowered for whom we go to for solid, time-tested values and guidance. Find a person whom you respect and admire whose feet you can sit at; this mentor will give you more than just help, leadership, and advice—often the hope and strength to persevere. Be a mentor when someone asks. It'll keep you on your game.

Love Is All

"I don't have time to even think about a mate, let alone date. Love? Forget it, I'm too busy!" You are human and, thus, need connection and love. You ever notice how advertising always seems to directly relate to this need? Do this, and you'll get the girl; wear that, and you'll get the guy. Our biological imperative as humans is to mate. You are human and need love. How much of your busyness is tangled up in circumventing love? Keeping yourself booked to the max with work, activities, and commitments is a convenient way to avoid connecting on a deeper level. Slow down and look around you to notice who's looking at you. The laws of attraction are all around you, so listen to your heart, not your bleeping PDA.

Contents Under Pressure

"People seem to respect and treat me better when they know how busy I am." You place too much pressure on yourself to perform. During a "busy epidemic," being called lazy might seem like the greatest insult. Placing overly high expectations on yourself and caring too much what others think leads to rigid perfectionism. When your basic needs are met, what's wrong with lowering your standards from perfect to "job well done"? What do you do that can be done by someone else? Who, outside of yourself, expects so much "busy" from you? Your pressure can be relieved when you separate reasonable expectations from the excessive demands of inflexible attention to detail.

Since You Can't Take It with You . . .

"The world is a mess. If we don't save it, who will?" You're searching for your legacy. Much of your busyness is probably a part of your efforts to make a mark on the world, something that says, "I was here, and I made a difference." At the core of your ultra-busy lifestyle is the heartfelt need to be significant. You live in a prosperous country with unlimited choices and the freedom to be whatever you want to be, and so you're going for it. Dear friend, this is a noble reason, but when you sacrifice other important parts of your life for the sake of your legacy, what have you gained? It is possible to take control of your busyness and still be significant.

Instant Payoff to Taming Your Busyness

Just because you know *why* you're so busy doesn't mean you've got an excuse to continue on your collision course to burnout. De-busifying is survival in today's world. It's a skill that allows your awareness of being too busy—and your ability to influence your level of busyness—to change significantly. Every time you reject the speed and intensity of which you've been living your life, you have de-busified. Take a look at the following list of pairs. Every time you choose the first over the last, you have de-busified:

▶ Peace over stress
▶ Balance over imbalance
▶ Happiness over sadness
▶ Simplification over complication
▶ Love over anger
▶ Function over dysfunction
▶ Joy over gloom
▶ Ease over pain
▶ Relationships over disharmony
▶ Satisfaction over frustration

It's not hard to tell when the de-busification has begun to work. When you de-busify, your thoughts will be optimistic, the words you say will have hope, your body will be loose and comfortable. Also, your employees will reflect and model your cheerful, good-natured disposition, and relationships with your family and friends will be more joyous and agreeable. But, best of all, you'll *be* a better person—from the inside out. In order to get there, though, you may have to abandon some of the excuses that people commonly use to justify their busyness.

Ten Popular Excuses for Being Too Busy

Everywhere you look you see busy people—rushed, harried, hassled, and exhausted. As you can probably tell by now,

I'm worried about them. I'm worried that they think their "busy" is going to get them what they want and need.

I'm worried that they make excuses for their busyness. These excuses are a halfhearted effort to explain why "busy" really isn't their fault. Making excuses is an obstacle to controlling busyness when they're made in place of earnest attempts to make the situation better. When you stop making excuses, you'll start making good.

"I Don't Have Enough Time to Do Everything Without Feeling Rushed"

Not true! You may believe you don't have enough time because you probably underestimate how long a task takes and overestimate how much you have to do. While it is true that you don't have time to do *everything*, you do have the same twenty-four hours in each day that Thomas Edison had. Time management starts with life management. Articulate your principles, values, and your mission in life, and then prioritize your activities accordingly.

Prioritize your to-do list and handle your high-value activities first so that unimportant busyness doesn't take over your life. The adage, "If you don't stand for something, you'll fall for anything," applies here. Stand up for something valuable and align your activities with your principles. Ask yourself, "What am I doing right now?" and "Is it in line with my values and what I believe to be important?" If you don't get to the end of your list, so what? You're living with purpose.

"Multitasking Automatically Makes Me More Efficient"

Busted! You don't have to look very far to see a jogger on his cell phone or the woman driving while eating lunch, on a conference call, and checking her makeup. We're all guilty of trying to shave time here and there. While doing so might save a few minutes, it can be downright dangerous to yourself and others. It's evident when people on the other end of the phone are distracted by replying to their e-mail or focused on some other busywork. You ask whether they're still on the line, and their responses sound disconnected and distant. When you're engaged in two or more tasks at once, you are not fully present for any of them.

Doing one thing at a time is a better use of your brain. Researchers at the Federal Aviation Administration and the University of Michigan found that working on numerous tasks at a time can take two to four times longer than if started one after the other. Brain scans of subjects multitasking show the brain constantly switching back and forth, using its neurons less efficiently. If you want to be more efficient, finish a task before moving on to the next, and you'll not only get it done faster and better, you'll get more benefit from the time you give your brain some downtime.

My very efficient and highly productive friend Nancy attributes her output to breaking any task or project into "chunks." She focuses on one "chunk" at a time, gets it done, and then moves to the next. It just looks like she's multitasking, when actually it's sequential tasking.

"Technology Simplifies My Life so I Can Do More"

Ha, ha, ha! Every new gadget or system touts how it's going to make your life easier and simpler. Technologies bring the world to us, and sadly, they also bring us to the world. Our senses are assaulted with more connections and information than the human soul can take in. In our efforts to filter out what we think isn't important or relevant to us, we are dulling ourselves. Our attention spans are shortening, and we block the very thing that can simplify our lives—peace and spiritual connection. The on/off switch is the best part of a new gadget because it gives you ultimate power. Just because technology allows you to be on-call all the time, that doesn't mean you have to be.

"Getting It All Done Will Make Me Happy"

Wrong! Recent scientific research has proven that happiness is not a goal but a process. Happiness brings success, not the other way around. Martin Seligman in *Authentic Happiness* says that happiness is pursuing a state of flow by engaging in activities that use your strengths and talents to serve others or participating in a cause that's bigger than yourself. You may complain—or boast—ceaselessly about being too busy, but in reality, this state of busyness just might be self-imposed. Your busyness must have a purpose in order for it to actually make you happy. Checking items off your checklist doesn't bring happiness in and of itself. That's just being busy for the sake of being busy.

"Working Double Overtime Is the Only Way I'll Get Ahead"

False! When you voluntarily and routinely expand your hours on the job, you are asking for more busyness. When your boss then knows that she can expect more hours from you, she piles on more responsibilities, thus creating a vicious cycle of more "busy." You'll garner more respect and forward movement in your career by the quality of your work than from the quantity of hours at your desk.

More often than not, fatigue, hunger, and low energy reduce your ability to think clearly and decrease your hand-eye coordination. You might end up less productive and more mistake-prone, leading to rework. All your busyness and lack of sleep may actually impact your reputation negatively. Your overachiever output might backfire when you're viewed as a kiss-ass by supervisors and colleagues. You also might be alienating yourself from your coworkers by setting the bar unreasonably high and making their output look poor.

"I'm Only Doing This for My Family"

Mistake! Spending extra hours at your job and bringing work home at night and on the weekends to support your family comes, ironically, at the expense of an optimum relationship with your family. No matter how many times you tell them you're doing it all for them, the message you're sending is different from your intention.

When you're tired, hassled, and overworked, you may miss milestones in the lives of your mate and children. Think twice before you say you're doing it for them. Trading family time for work time may irreparably harm your relationships with your family. They may think that you love your work more than them since you devote so much time to it. You're conveying that your job is more important to you than they are. To make matters worse, you might be setting them up to dread their own future! If they think that "work" is a four-letter word, they might decide to stay a kid forever and avoid it if they can.

Sometimes your loved ones blame themselves for your overworking—that if somehow they were better or smarter, you wouldn't have to work so hard. This kind of guilt repels people from the contributory factor—you. This self-blame may trigger strong emotions that are very painful. Often, they may find it easier to deal with these emotions by tuning you out or "running away" from you.

"I Have to Catch Up Financially"

Not right! News of the economy tanking is enough to shake anyone. Practically everyone is in a panic about money these days, talking about how bad the economy is and what might happen if things don't turn around. This kind of panic is contagious, so you step up your pace and take on extra tasks. You buy into the mind-set that you've got to do more to make money. Instead, consider doing the following:

▶ Concentrate on the job you have and do it very well so you're a valued member of the team (and less apt to be downsized or off-shored).

▶ Review your personal budget (or make one for the first time) and be realistic about how much you've got coming in and going out.

▶ Focus on where you can trim back, clean up your credit, and save.

▶ Plan how to get a better job by continuing your education.

A survey of millionaires shows that they don't use time as a measurement of success. They measure their success based on their output quality, the results. Sometimes less really is more.

"My Friends Expect Me to Be Too Busy to See Them Most of the Time"

Not true! Skipping seeing your friends or begging off non-work activities because you're too busy (or tired) is a big mistake. Longtime pals and friendly coworkers are the key to your support system in tough times. Like a garden that once flourished, your friendships need to be tended, or they go fallow when you most need them. You may not know your coworker's been distracted or unreasonable because of family problems if you didn't attend the optional department sack lunch meeting.

When your friend says, "I didn't want to bother you, you're always so busy," it is not a compliment! Especially when you find out something you might have missed while you were too busy working. It doesn't take too long for your friends to grasp the futility of inviting you out: "She's always busy." "He'd never go last minute."

You might think you're being more efficient by cutting out fun and socializing, but you may be avoiding—or pushing away—relationships that could help you do things easier or better. Slow down and have a good giggle—or cry—with a friend. If you can't visit, at least stay in touch with a heartfelt note or card saying how much you value their friendship.

"It's OK That I'm Too Busy—Everyone's Too Busy"

Do not pass go! This is not an Olympic event you need to train for, and there is no great award or endorsement deal if you win the "I'm busier than you" race. Just because the world is busy moving at warp speed around you doesn't mean it's good or right for you. It's difficult to *not* feel the need to get competitive with being busy. It takes attention and effort to *not* succumb to the busyness plague and spread it around.

It only takes one person to be the calm in the center of the rush, the voice of reason that says "no" to more busyness, or the smile that lifts someone else's heart. It's far nobler to stand out for your sensibility than for your speed. You're bright—why couldn't you be the first in your group with a new, less-busy, and more relaxed lifestyle? You'll actually be living a green lifestyle—natural, sustainable, and reducing the negative impact on health.

"At Least I'm Not Bored"

Incorrect! Parents say that if they don't keep their kids busy, they will get bored and sit around eating junk and playing video games. You think that you are staying away from boredom by being chronically busy. Busy and bored can be different descriptions of the same problem—feeling like you aren't completely engaged with high-quality experiences. These are mental processes that loop each other like a Venn diagram.

Filling every minute with activity and planning every day to accomplish the most doesn't leave much room for wonder, serendipity, chance, and just plain magic. You need to create space, or gaps, in your activity continuum. Space spares processing resources in your brain to be open to a brilliant solution. Space invites serendipity and unexpected blessings by allowing you to be more aware of your surroundings.

You've Taken Responsibility, Now Take a Bow!

I believe that you have just done a very courageous act—you've taken responsibility for your busyness by closely examining your reasons for being so busy. Bravo! You may have also discovered that some of your reasons are actually excuses, and that some of your excuses are actually myths. Your next heroic and spirited act is to declare that you don't want or need the stress that your busyness is causing you. Read the next chapter to find out which of your physical symptoms and emotional warning signs are pointing to dangerous stress levels and learn a quick, easy, five-minute first aid for beating stress. This is your life, and you're making it better.

Chapter 3

The Dangers of Being Too Busy

Nothing can bring you
peace but yourself.

—Ralph Waldo Emerson

Being busy may be a necessary part of your job and your life, but being too busy has more than just social consequences. As you'll discover in this chapter, it's not the busyness itself that ends up getting the best of you, it's the stress that comes with the territory that proves to be most problematic. If you keep up the hectic, action-packed pace that probably led you to pick up this book, inevitably you will begin feeling the physical and mental signs of stress. That's right, my friends: being too busy is bad for your health. When you start to feel trapped by your lifestyle, you're in the "busyness danger zone."

Pat and Dawn

This is the tale of two ladies. As in Charles Dickens's *A Tale of Two Cities*, it begins with the best of times and the worst of times, so to speak. Dawn and Pat have similar full-time positions as retirement community managers across town from each other. Each has a husband with a full-time job, and they have children of a similar age. These women's days are jammed with meetings, activities, and obligations.

Similarities in their days end when you see the way each of them handles her busyness. Pat is clearly on the brink of a breakdown. Dawn, however, gets just as much done, but she doesn't have the frazzled look and short-fuse reaction that Pat does. Since neither one of them has the luxury of getting rid of any of her obligations, the difference is how each of them handles her ensuing stress.

Dawn's day begins forty minutes before the rest of her family wakes up. She calls this "sacred private time." She does some light stretching, gets a cup of coffee that was set to brew automatically before she woke up, and gets ready for work, using her shower time to review the day ahead and say some positive affirmations. Her husband, twelve-year-old, and teenager scuttle through their morning preparations that began the night before when the day's schedule was worked out. When leaving the house, everyone grabs his or her respective backpack or bag sitting by the door. They've learned that when the car is idling in the driveway, Mom will leave on time with or without them. During Dawn's one-hour commute, she listens to the latest book on tape from her favorite author. At work, she often takes a "walking" lunch and has a method for handling copious e-mails and voice mails. At home she enlists the entire family to pull their own weight in housekeeping and occasionally puts her foot down to more evening commitments.

Even with a similar job, commute, and family structure, Pat's days start chaotic and only get worse as she juggles her workload and home demands. She is known for always being late even though she works late and through lunch most days. It's hard to find what she needs on her desk, and a recent hard drive crash nearly got her fired when she admitted that she hadn't backed up as requested. It's easy to see the stress in her face, hear the tension in her voice, and she's exhausted by her own admission.

The difference between these women is that Dawn has a plan for handling all she needs to do at work and home, while Pat doesn't. Dawn controls her stress level a little each day, while Pat figures she'll catch up someday—which never seems to happen.

Stress Myths

In the 1920s, you wouldn't even know what the term "stressed-out" meant, unless you were an engineer talking about the intensity force that one body makes upon another. In the 1930s, Hans Selye, a clumsy young Canadian doctor, discovered that his tendency to drop his lab rats and the ensuing chase to trap them caused them to develop ulcers and to shrink their immune tissues. Selye adopted the word "stress" to describe the rats' life under tension. His definition of stress is "the nonspecific response of the body to any demand made on it when external demands exceed resources." While the existence of stress in modern society is unquestionable, some of the so-called facts floating around about stress are less so. Here are some myths about stress that need to go away:

Myth #1: In an ideal world, there wouldn't be any stress.
Truth: Too little stress—boredom—can make you as miserable as too much stress.

Myth #2: Only unpleasant situations are stressful.
Truth: Falling in love can be as stressful as breaking up, and coming into money can be as stressful as losing your job.

Myth #3: My stress would disappear if I could quit my job/get divorced/grow up/get my degree/this person would leave my life.
Truth: Stress is not "out there." It's something we create by interpreting situations and reacting in our own way.

Myth #4: Busyness doesn't hurt you; get over it.
Truth: A persistent state of alarm from being ultra-busy, and all the extra hassles that come with it, are more harmful than one stressful event.

Myth #5: Exercise is the best stress reducer.
Truth: The best stress-reducing strategies call for exercise along with relaxation techniques, healthful nutritional choices, social support, and professional help. If you think exercise alone will keep you safe from the dangers of stress—think again!

Testing the Impact of Stress on Your Health

Some degree of busyness is a fact of modern-day working life, but you can take steps to manage the impact your busyness has on you. These steps can range from something as simple as walking during lunch or practicing deep-breathing exercises every hour to investing in cognitive-behavioral therapy, a psychotherapeutic approach shown to successfully reduce stress, depression, and anxiety. Before you decide what actions to take to reduce your stress, though, it's important to evaluate your stress response in three areas:

▶ Life events
▶ Physical symptoms
▶ Emotional indicators

Your Life Events

The mind-body connection is not a new concept; science has long been studying the effects of cumulative life events on not only your mentality but your physiology. As an organism, the human body is fairly hearty, but even a champion prizefighter will drop from multiple, successive blows. Note whether the following experiences have happened to you in the last two years. There are no right or wrong answers. You'll also notice that not all the events are negative. (This quiz is based on my contemporary adaptation of the Holmes-Rahe Stress Scale, which was originally published in 1967.)

Place a check mark after each and calculate your score.

☐	Death of spouse or life partner	100
☐	Death of family member	80
☐	Severe personal injury or illness	60
☐	Loss of job	60
☐	Divorce or separation	50
☐	Foreclosure on home	50
☐	Marriage or marriage reconciliation	45
☐	Change in health of family member	40
☐	Death of close friend	40
☐	Pregnancy in household	40
☐	Change of career	40
☐	Sexual troubles	35
☐	More arguments with spouse, partner	35
☐	Child leaving home	30
☐	Outstanding achievement or award	25

☐	Change of residence	20
☐	Change of sleeping or eating habits	20
☐	Vacation	10
	Total	____

Scoring

0–149	**No significant problem**
150–199	**Slight crisis**, 33 percent chance of getting stress-related illness
200–299	**Moderate crisis**, 50 percent chance of getting stress-related illness
300+	**Major life crisis**, 80 percent chance of serious physical illness in next two years

Many of these situations are negative situations where stress is expected, but you may not crumble under the weight of these terrible events. Your stress increases exponentially the more life events you have to deal with, though, and you need to be aware of this reality.

Your Physical Symptoms

These are in-your-face signs that your busyness is starting to cross over from efficiency to stressful. They are easy to evaluate because they are obvious. Perhaps people have even pointed them out to you. Busyness is often contagious, and your colleagues or kids might mirror them back at you by exhibiting similar symptoms. In tight-knit groups or loyal workplaces, it's hard to identify which came first—symptoms of being too busy or acting like someone else who is too busy. The result is the same: your body is taking the brunt of your busyness.

The following quiz is distilled from my firsthand experience with thousands of people in stress classes over the past twenty years and personal interviews I've conducted with overbusy, overwhelmed women and men.

Place a check mark beside what you have experienced in the past six months.

☐   Frequent headaches, dizziness

☐   Stiff neck, backaches

☐   Heart racing or pounding in ears or throat

☐   Dry mouth with cold hands and feet

☐   Muscle spasms, tightness

☐   Loss of weight

☐   Overeating, bingeing

☐   Diarrhea, indigestion, nausea

☐   Fatigue, exhaustion

☐   Insomnia, nightmares, or problems sleeping

☐   Frequently "under the weather"

☐   Increased alcohol, stimulants, smoking

☐   Nervousness

☐   Tension in face or jaw

☐   Leg jiggling or foot tapping

☐ Hair twirling, pulling, tossing

☐ Excessive talking, interrupting, giggling

Number of check marks: _____

Scoring

0 to 5 You're probably managing your stress well.

6 to 11 You're probably feeling stress so frequently that it seems normal.

11+ Your stress is out of control and needs serious intervention.

Your physical symptoms are signs that your body is reacting to—or rebelling against—how you are handling your life. They are not just symptoms of general stress but a sign that your immunity—your resistance to infection or disease and your response to biochemical, environmental, and psychosocial factors—is being challenged.

Your Emotional Indicators

Your emotional state says a lot about how you're handling your busyness. All of us have a variety of emotions, and we needn't worry about the occasional overreaction. The key to which of these emotions you feel or exhibit is not that you feel them but the frequency, intensity, and duration of these emotions. Professional mental health care providers use a manual published by the American Psychiatric Association called the *Diagnostic and Statistical Manual of Mental*

Disorders, currently in its fourth edition (*DSM-IV*). They are instructed to become concerned when five or more of the following symptoms of depression are present for most of the day nearly every day for at least two weeks.

Which, if any, of these symptoms are you now experiencing?

▶ Irritability with friends and loved ones
▶ Anger at little things or certain people
▶ Temper outbursts or road rage
▶ Escapism or the desire to run away
▶ Memory loss, mental gridlock, or brain fog
▶ Feeling frustrated or discouraged
▶ Inability to make a decision
▶ Feelings of unworthiness or shame
▶ Negativity or resentment
▶ Unfinished grieving for a loss
▶ Loss of attention or concentration
▶ Hypochondria
▶ Feeling down or ready tears
▶ Anxiety or a feeling of impending doom
▶ Resignation to difficult situations

If you have five or more of these symptoms along with persistently sad and empty feelings for two or more weeks, please get professional help. See a mental health care provider or your primary care doctor, as most cases of depression will not be helped by stress reduction alone.

As you can see, excess stress has a powerfully negative effect on your life—physically, mentally, and emotionally. Read on to learn a simple, easy, and quick way to counteract the little stresses before they deplete your natural resources. The following exercise can be used any place or time—except when operating heavy machinery or driving a car—and as often as you want, without unpleasant side effects.

Five-Minute First Aid

Under certain conditions, a small cut on your arm could kill
you—for instance, if the cut was in an artery and you were
anemic, in which case your blood wouldn't clot, and you
could do nothing to stop it. Likewise, everyday busyness
leads to stress, which can lead to potentially life-threatening
health problems if you're not careful. Luckily, there are
several small adjustments you can make that will stave off
these health problems. That's why I'm giving you a powerfully simple first-aid tool for your antistress kit. As with a
pressure-relief valve (or the little jiggler on top of a pressure
cooker), benefits of this exercise are immediate. It is faster
and longer acting than popping a pill and without the lin-
gering consequences of a tequila shot.

I've been teaching this five-minute first aid at my workshops for many years to men and women of all ages and
from a variety of work and life positions. No matter if my
topic focus is dealing with difficult people, gender conflicts, or stress reduction, I always throw this exercise into
the mix. I get e-mails, letters, and comments from people
telling me that it works so well that they now incorporate
it into their lives and teach it to others. Several managers have taught it to their staff and have taken to hand-
ing out their own version of a "first-aid pass" that gives a
worker permission to take a five-minute first-aid break *now*.
Another manager of a particularly stressed-out department
turned an unused closet into an SFA (stress first-aid) room—
complete with chair, pleasant posters, light switch, and an
"occupied/available" sign on the door.

Bonnie runs her own catering business, often with
more than twenty people working for her on a job. She
started using this process when she found herself hyper-
ventilating and nauseated while working with one particular high-profile "bridezilla" who could potentially influence

many more jobs. Bonnie confessed in a letter to me later that she came incredibly close to losing her cool with the young woman (and her mother), but then she locked herself in the bathroom and applied this five-minute first aid. She was able to pull herself together, resolve the hovering difficult situation, and even get all the people involved laughing and lightening up.

While you might not always have as much at stake as there was with Bonnie, this exercise can be very helpful since your health is at stake in the long run. Do this exercise whenever you need immediate pressure relief. If you're too busy and you find yourself on the verge of becoming stressed-out, it's time for your five-minute first aid!

Go to a place where you won't be disturbed. (Trust me, unless it's a dire emergency, the world will survive without you.) Bring an eight-ounce glass of water at room temperature.

1. Loosen any constricting clothing, such as a tie, neckline, waistband, or belt. (Go ahead, nobody's looking.)
2. Drink your water.
3. Sit in a chair with your feet flat on the ground and close your eyes. Put your hands in your lap or hang them loosely at your sides.
4. While allowing your stomach to "pooch out," take deep, slow breaths. Inhale through your nose and exhale slowly through your mouth. Repeat ten times.
5. Starting at your toes, "tighten" and hold them tightly for a count of ten. Move slowly and concentrate only on the muscles that you're tightening.
6. You are now going to be moving upward on your body, holding the "tighten" step for a count of ten. When you're finished with each body part, inhale and exhale slowly:

▶ Tighten and relax your calves.
▶ Push your knees together tightly and release.
▶ Tighten your buttocks and release.
▶ Tighten your stomach and release.
▶ Squeeze your fists tightly and release.
▶ Flex your biceps and release.
▶ Squeeze your upper body with your arms and release.
▶ Scrunch your shoulders toward your ears and release.
▶ Crumple your whole face and relax.

7. Drop your head to your chest slowly. Inhale as you roll your head to the left until it is hanging backward with your jaw loose. Exhale as you slowly roll toward your right shoulder, then back to the starting position. Repeat, rolling from the right to the left slowly.

8. Open your eyes and stretch like a cat waking up. Stand up slowly. Align yourself as if there is a string pulling you straight up from the ground.

You might feel a little groggy or "spacey" right after you complete this stress first aid, which is completely normal. Walk slowly with good posture and continue to breathe slowly and evenly. You will feel refreshed and alert again in a short time.

Calling Dr. Heart

Early in my nursing career, I worked in the intensive care unit at a small community hospital. Along with the standard duties we performed for patients in the unit, we were also responsible for responding when a patient "crashed"— their breathing or heart stopped, or they had a sudden loss of consciousness. Instead of hollering for help, someone picked up the phone and alerted the hospital opera-

tor. She got on the PA system and called for help. So the
entire hospital wasn't alarmed by, "Patient trying to die
on us in Room 301," a certain code was used instead: "Dr.
Heart to Room 301." I'd sprint to the room to take over the
resuscitation until a physician arrived. Hospitals and medical centers today still have dedicated crash teams whose
sole purpose is to save those patients who are in the most
immediate danger.

The symptoms of depression are important but the following are urgent symptoms that you're "crashing" and in
immediate danger. According to the *DSM-IV*, professional
help should be sought *immediately* if you have one or more
of these symptoms:

- Persistent thoughts of suicide or dying
- Attempts to commit suicide
- Panic attacks
- Trouble swallowing or catching breath; fainting
- Feeling of imminent death
- New or worse anxiety or depression
- Acting on dangerous impulses
- Unusual changes in behavior or mood

Although no single cause of depression has been identified, it appears that interaction among genetic, biochemical, environmental, and psychosocial factors may play a
role. The fact is, depression is not a personal weakness or a
condition that can be willed or wished away, but it can be
successfully treated.

An estimated 33 to 35 million U.S. adults are likely to
experience depression at some point during their lifetime.
The disease affects men and women of all ages, races, and
economic levels. However, women are at a significantly
greater risk than men to develop major depression. Studies

show that episodes of depression occur twice as frequently in women as in men. Although anyone can develop depression, some types of depression, including major depression, seem to run in families. Whether or not depression is genetic, the disorder is believed to be associated with changes to levels of chemicals in the brain, such as seratonin and norephinephrine.

Many people cite financial concerns to explain why they don't seek help for their mental health. Today mental health professionals usually practice cognitive-behavioral therapy (CBT). CBT has been shown to help ease symptoms of depression and anxiety more quickly than five-day-a-week analysis and is widely accepted as a cost-effective way to treat psychopathology. Check your company's HR or employee assistance program for low-cost (or free) counseling services. You can call your local public health department or hospital for referral ideas or use a psychiatric nurse-practitioner. And don't forget that your church or synagogue may offer counseling with a sliding-scale payment schedule.

Beware of *Karoshi*!

So now you know how stress from your busyness is affecting you. Its consequences range from making you slightly uncomfortable or irritable to miserable, overwhelmed, or severely debilitated. Continuing unchecked, it will cause physical problems threatening your life—high blood pressure, heart disease, asthma attacks, headaches, and increased susceptibility to viruses and colds. In the extreme, even death!

A recently coined word in Japan, *karoshi*, translates to "death from stress of overwork"! The Japanese don't have the market cornered on life-threatening stress, though. It's just as pervasive in America. The American Institute of

Stress and the National Council on Compensation Insurance, Inc., recently reported the following:

- ▶ As many as 90 percent of visits to primary care physicians are about stress.
- ▶ Approximately 750,000 attempted suicides per year are related to stress.
- ▶ Up to 80 percent of industrial accidents are due to stress.
- ▶ One million people a day are absent due to stress, causing $200 billion in absenteeism, workers' compensation claims, and health insurance.
- ▶ It is estimated that 40 percent of employee turnover is stress related.
- ▶ Stress accounts for $26 billion in medical and disability payments and $95 billion in lost productivity per year.

Keep a check on your chronic busyness. You may not realize the toll it takes on your health until it's too late. A frog would never willingly put itself into a pot of boiling hot water, but it would relax in a nice warm pot of water that gradually got hotter and eventually boiled. That is what your busyness is like. It gradually propels you forward until you're in a persistent state of alarm, which then causes stress symptoms to manifest physically, mentally, and emotionally.

Sound the Alarm!

The human body developed our fight-or-flight reaction, or defense mechanisms, to deal with the threat of predators and aggressors. Cavemen either killed the saber-toothed tiger that showed up on their land or fled for the hills if they thought they were in danger. Thousands of years later, we humans still have these same response patterns in our day-to-day world. Your reality of managing a job, making ends meet, and taking care of your family is full of new threats.

It makes sense that your body automatically kicks into high gear when you are facing a physical threat. A tiny part of your brain called the *hypothalamus* sets off a series of alarm signals to your adrenal glands, which are located on top of your kidneys, to release adrenaline and cortisol. The alarm signal also goes out to parts of your brain controlling mood, motivation, and fear, and that part of your brain in turn delivers a fight-or-flight reaction.

Here's the catch-22 of your highly complex alarm system. Your body doesn't distinguish between physical threats (that saber-toothed tiger) and psychological threats (work problems, life changes, overwhelming busyness). This problem is compounded since psychological threats tend to be prolonged. Your alarm system is intended for short-term crisis and not for long periods of time. It's like when you push your gas pedal to the floor while passing a car. The engine roars into a different gear, and it gains power and speed. Like trying to keep your car in the red zone, if you continually have your alarm system on, you risk permanently damaging your engine.

Being Too Busy Not Only Makes You Sick, It Makes You Old!

The National Academy of Sciences reported the direct link between stress, aging, and growing old before your time. Researchers at the University of California, San Francisco, studied mothers caring for chronically ill children. They were otherwise healthy and between the ages of twenty and fifty. It was found that these women's chronic stress hastened the shriveling of certain genes inside cells—shortening their life span and speeding the body's deterioration.

In one year, they had undergone the equivalent of ten years of additional aging!

This study demonstrates on a molecular level there is no such thing as separation of mind and body. Dr. Dennis Novack, a researcher with the Drexel University College of Medicine, reported that your very molecules respond to your psychological situation. If you're in peril from stress on a cellular level, the big picture isn't pretty either. The *New England Journal of Medicine* reported on the physical price your body pays when you make accommodations to stress. The concept of "allostatic load," coined by Bruce S. McEwen at the Rockefeller University, points out that chronic stress creates a slow and steady cascade of harm to your health involving the brain and the body. Consequences of allostatic load can include the altering of the response of your adrenal glands in releasing hormones, which, when unchecked, can result in hypertension.

The stress resulting from busyness is an equal-opportunity syndrome. It used to be thought that women have better stress-coping mechanisms from their tendency to talk things over with friends. As recently as the early 1990s, men got more stress-related diseases. Studies showed it was because they were expected to be strong, self-reliant, successful, and all-knowing—in control and solving their problems alone.

Today, women not only share stress-related diseases equally with men but they also react worse to trauma. Women are more likely to suffer depression, have a higher risk of developing Alzheimer's, and the risk for PTSD (post-traumatic stress disorder) following a trauma is twice as high in women. Most impressive is a fifty-two-country study of more than twenty-four thousand people, examining stress at home and at work, financial stress, and stress surrounding major life events. It found that stress raised heart attack risk by 250 percent, almost as much as smoking and diabetes.

Reboot Your Life

When your busyness gets out of hand, your body needs to recover and reset the stress response. Your body does this by releasing endorphins to stabilize your hormone levels. But if stressful situations persist and your body is continually forced into the alert mode, it is like plugging too many power tools into one electrical outlet. The drain is too much, and eventually you blow the circuit breaker.

It is impossible to live completely free of stress when you're as busy as a modern-day lifestyle demands, but you can prevent some stress and minimize the impact when it can't be avoided. You may feel like you have no choice but to accept that a stressful level of busyness is a necessary part of your job and your life. You may feel trapped. Many women I've interviewed have been unable to delegate their duties enough to take a much-needed vacation. They've told me, "I can't fire my family," and "I don't want to walk away from my business."

I believe that many times it's not just being too busy that ends up getting the best of you, it's your feeling of hopelessness about the situation. To this, I say, "Relax!" This book will teach you how to eliminate some of your busyness and change your perception of and reaction to the stress that comes with it. Take a deep breath and let it out very slowly. Now that you realize the dangers of your current lifestyle, are you ready to make a change? That's the good news. Read on and follow the exercises, and in no time at all, you'll bring new vitality, balance, fun, and a sense of purpose into your life.

Chapter 4

Preparing to Leave the "Island of Too Busy"

Please give me some advice in your next letter. I promise not to take it.

—Edna St. Vincent Millay

t wasn't until the birth of her daughter that time-management expert Julie Morgenstern felt that her right-brained, creative style of living was anything that needed changing. She had never suffered for this until one beautiful spring afternoon when she decided to take her child out for her first waterfront stroll. After two and a half hours of gathering everything that she needed for the trip, her daughter was asleep, and Julie had missed "the moment." The chance for the first walk had passed, but more important, she realized that if she didn't change her cluttered and chaotic lifestyle, her child was never going to see the light of day.

How many "moments" have you missed? You might not even know, because you probably manage to pull things off most of the time. In the past, you somehow have always found the keys, made the deadline, got the tickets, or balanced the budget. Sometimes we can get so busy and wrapped up in the tasks at hand, coming one after the other, that the truly important moments in life can sort of pass us by.

You picked up this book because "too busy" isn't working for you anymore. You want off the "Island of Too Busy." No quick trip to the organizing store or day at the spa is going to de-busify your life. De-busifying isn't like putting a cast on a broken arm. It's building a new, bionic arm that is stronger, more capable, and unbreakable. It's a journey to look at your life at work and at home and to acquire skills to prevent your excessive busyness from ruining your job, your health, and your relationships. This journey will empower you and make you happier, healthier, and freer.

Admit Your Chaos

You may be overbusy and wanting a change, or you might be what I call "happy overbusy." All the parts of your life you love, but the sheer amount of tasks you must accomplish has pushed you into overdrive.

Eventually, after going with your pedal to the metal for too long, your life begins to unravel. Whether you're running around for your children, closing the deal of a lifetime, or frantic with charity work, it doesn't justify what it does to your body and soul. At some point things start falling through the cracks—you forget a meeting, lose a vital document, and you miss "moments." Then the unexpected or unscheduled vitally needs your attention—your sister needs chemo, your parents have to move to assisted living, or your company moves across the country.

If you're going to leave all this behind and get away from the "Island of Too Busy," you have to take the first step. Like the first step of any recovery program, you must admit that you are powerless against the forces that be. You're alive in this moment, working this job, being a member of this family, living in this world. It is what it is, and you will have to admit that your life is chaotic and possibly spinning out of control. That's it. Say it: "I'm too busy." You might even start feeling better already by simply admitting it to yourself.

Make Yourself the Priority

On your path to busyness, you decided that doing for others was the top priority and doing for yourself was less important. Or you got so enamored with the praise and rewards for getting things done that you pushed your own needs away. Somewhere along the line, requirements for your body and the desires of your heart became unimportant, irrelevant, or insignificant.

If you're going to take the journey away from busyness, you'll have to get over the guilt of making yourself a priority; you must give yourself permission to structure your life around de-busifying. Examining and adjusting your people-pleasing habits is not a revival of a "me movement," but rather a return to a centered and balanced lifestyle.

Decide you deserve it. If you don't, your efforts in life will continue yielding negative returns. Imagine your energy as an account that you've been withdrawing from. If you don't take time for yourself, you'll become emotionally and physically bankrupt. Consider these scenarios:

- ▶ One minute spent refusing an errand necessitated by someone else's forgetfulness could yield thirty minutes to read your favorite magazine.
- ▶ The five-minute first aid outlined in Chapter 3 might relax you into solving a baffling problem.
- ▶ Thirty minutes planning your meals yields better meals that boost your immune system and a less hectic dinnertime.
- ▶ One hour walking and gabbing with a dear friend yields endorphins that improve your attitude with a difficult in-law.
- ▶ One cell-phone-free day of being physically active with your children yields a restful night's sleep.
- ▶ A one-week vacation yields renewed energy to finish a yearlong project with creativity and pizzazz and erases the stress lines from your face.

Join the de-busifying movement. Start building up your energy account now by making deposits in it so you can get it working for you later.

You Have Choices

An ancient legend says that Hercules was irritated by a strange-looking animal that blocked his path in a threatening manner. Hercules struck it with his club in anger. As he went on his way, he encountered the same creature again several times, and in each instance, the beast grew larger and more fearsome than before. At last, a heavenly messenger appeared and warned Hercules to stop his furious assaults, saying, "The monster is Strife, and you are stirring it up. Just let it alone, and it will shrivel and cease to trouble you."

When you see Strife in your path, you can change your perspective and look at it as a good thing. It's a change for the positive, because making a choice increases your personal power and reduces Strife's effect on you. The sooner you identify your problem and make a choice about how to deal with it, the more control you'll have.

These are your basic choices when you are problem solving:

▶ You can tolerate the situation. (a.k.a. making do, wishful thinking, suffering in silence, or complaining to anyone who'll listen)

▶ You can remove yourself from the situation. (a.k.a. quitting the job, leaving the committee, hanging up the phone, deleting the message, or going to your mental quiet place)

▶ You can change the situation. *Yes, you can!* (a.k.a.
  stand up to the bully, change your response to the
  complainer, refuse to accept more tasks, change your
  behavior, renegotiate the agreement)

When you know your weaknesses, hot buttons, and
your personal communication style, you can get back your
power and internal peace. What seems like the best outcome for *you*?

Use Your VISA on this Journey

When you travel to a foreign country, you need permission
for entry. This official stamp in your passport granting entry
for a specific purpose and a finite amount of time is known
as a visa. Before you enter the strange and unfamiliar country where you decrease (or eliminate) your busyness, you
need a different kind of visa. It's valid whenever and wher-
ever you need to start decreasing your "busy"—and for as
long as you need it.

Use this VISA when you begin your journey. I know that
you are too busy to learn complex formulas, so I'm going to
make it simple and easy to begin the process of debusifying
your life.

V Visualize clearly a time in your life when you were
    happy or content. The goal is to clearly see in your
mind's eye where you were physically, mentally, and emotionally and what you were thinking, feeling, and experiencing. It's important to involve as many of your senses
as possible so that you make this state of being freely and
easily accessible. What do you see? Who is with you? What
does your body feel like? If this is difficult, you can picture
someone who represents what you want or whom you want

to emulate. This image or feeling becomes the touchstone of your journey; the replication of that contentment is what you're going for when you de-busify.

I **Investigate** your busyness with a bright light. Take a truthful look at the people and activities that either contribute to or contaminate your life. Contaminators could be high-maintenance pals at work, high-drama friends, neighbors who seem unwilling or unable to honor boundaries, volunteering too much for extra credit, and taking on others' problems. Contributors might be the friend who is a shining example of how you want to handle your family, a mentor who freely helps you through perplexing work situations, the hobby that is energizing to you, or the foundation for a noble cause.

Don't wait for a devastating experience to occur before you start making changes to your lifestyle. Don't let your priorities and balance become so skewed that you return home to an empty house when your mate leaves you or go into cardiac arrest when your poor heart becomes officially overburdened.

S **Strategize.** Take some time to plan how you're going to slow down and find some purpose to your busyness. Design your life so it has some open space for giving thanks, doing good, and investing in others. To start, write down how you use every fifteen-minute time block for two weeks. Be sure to be as detailed as possible—traffic jams, daydreaming, online surfing, television—all of it. Don't make any judgments or changes. You just need to log your time. Now, notice how you *really* use your time rather than how you *mean* to use it. In later chapters, you will use this time journal as an aid in learning detailed strategies for rebalancing your life.

You are going to plan out your strategy with happiness as your eventual goal. In their groundbreaking book *How We Chose to Be Happy*, Rick Foster and Greg Hicks call "the intention to be happy . . . the most hidden, yet powerful choice we make" in our adventure of happiness. They go on to explain that our intention is a powerful driving force because it is fully in our control. According to them, our intentions are "internal messages we give ourselves that dictate what we say, how we say it, and how we see things." Make happiness your intention when you begin to strategize the changes in your life.

A **Action!** Get busy, but not necessarily by putting more stuff on your plate. Perhaps it's getting busy *not* doing something or actively working into your schedule some time for *doing nothing*. My Texan friend says, "When you've got to eat a frog, don't look at it too long." When you are facing as daunting a task as de-busifying your life, don't spend too much time thinking about the enormity or impossibility of it. A plan will only get you so far until you put it into action. So just set your mind to it and get going.

Now that you've declared that the "Island of Too Busy" is not your happy place and you agree to make yourself a priority, let's get started making your life better. You have the power to enlighten your workspace and make yourself less busy at work. You not only have the power, but you're worth it. Since you know what it is you have to do now, the next step is putting it into action and making work *work* for you.

Part 2

Work Is Great, Except I'm So Busy

Chapter 5

Strategies for Working Smarter, Not Harder

Being busy does not always mean real work. Seeming to do is not doing.

—Thomas Edison

D id you pick up this book because your job is the source of so much busyness in your life? Here's a blast of cold water in your face: they call it "work" for a reason! The reality is that your work will often suck the life out of you (or it will just plain suck). No matter how much you love your job, sometimes it is going to feel like pure busywork. Even the best, most creative, and most fulfilling jobs will not be fun at times. The secret to making it better is to change or fix the things you can—and deal with the rest—while you're there, so you can make the most out of your life when you are *not* there.

You are working smarter when you make your workspace more efficient and comfortable, streamline your e-mail and voice mail, polish some work habits, and institute a few time-savers. That is what you're going to learn in this chapter. Working smarter automatically decreases your busyness, and when you reduce your busyness, your body will be energized, your attitude lighter, and your outlook brighter. Don't you feel smarter already?

Enlightening Your Workspace

We start here because an efficient and pleasant work environment is really the foundation for the rest of the changes outlined in this chapter. If your physical work life is in disarray, there are very few tips or strategies that will prove very effective to reduce your busyness. Start the de-busification of your work life fresh, by making sure your workspace is working for you, not against you.

Conquer the Clutter

A cluttered workspace is *not* the sign of a creative mind. It's the sign of a stressed-out, overbusy person. Having an organized office with a clear filing system and your work tools handy, right where you look for them, can save *hours* of time. One recent study reported that nurses spent *twice as much time* looking for an object as using it for their patients. It's frightening to think that your nurse spends more time looking for instruments than taking care of you. And if you think that nurses are the only ones looking for their equipment, think again. The time you spend searching around your desk for binder clips or hunting for that important file could be better spent on any number of tasks.

Your first order is to bring simplicity and organization to your workspace. You must be *ruthless* in doing so, but when you have a clean and orderly area to work from, you'll be glad you were. A neat work area will not only save you time looking for things, but it will also quietly inject some serenity into your hectic day. Perhaps surprisingly, you just might find your attitude becoming a reflection of your uncluttered surroundings. These quick tips will get you started:

▶ Make as much open space as you can on your desk surface. Only leave necessary items out and one personal item (photo, bobblehead doll, action figure).
▶ Clean the desktop on your computer, leaving icons for programs used.
▶ Clean your file cabinets—toss or store elsewhere files not used in a year or longer.

- ▶ Purge your reference books, catalogs, phone books; toss if it's somewhere else (online, conference room, computer).
- ▶ Get accordion files or hanging folders.
- ▶ Set up the most efficient filing system for your needs (alphabetized, sorted by geography, etc.).
- ▶ Touch a piece of paper or file only one time—once it's in your hands, toss or deal with it *now* rather than create another pile of deal-with-later items.
- ▶ Get in the habit of having (and using) two trash cans; fill one up, put it to the side, and then fill the other.
- ▶ Buy a shredder for purging documents with sensitive information and junk mail that may contain business or personal information.
- ▶ To help the environment, recycle paper, bottles, and cans as you purge.

Renovate Your Ergonomics

You may not be aware of your body position when you're on the computer, on the phone, or reaching for a file. You may think that the short periods of time you're twisting to see your monitor, leaning over to answer the phone, or being hunched over your keyboard don't matter. Those moments add up to backaches, headaches, and stiff necks that aggravate your busyness. These aches accumulate and lurk in the background of your busyness, slowly draining your energy and making everything seem to take longer.

It isn't necessary to "feng shui" your office, unless you are already a big fan of this ancient Chinese practice of creating harmonious environments and want your office in tune with your "chi." I do believe that being mindful of ergonomics helps free you of those little insults that can happen to your body and soul while you work. You don't have to redecorate the entire floor to your liking—and the odds are that you wouldn't be allowed to anyway—but there are some subtle changes you can make in your office or cubicle that will make a big difference. Here are the basics:

Desk. If you want to discourage interruptions, face it away from the door and have a mirror on your wall or desk that frees you from having to turn to check visitor arrival. Sometimes people will poke their heads in your office to see if you "look busy." With your desk facing the opposite direction, you will always look busy because nobody will be able to catch your eye without knocking or calling out your name. If people can't catch your eye, they can't snag your mind. If you work in a cubicle, let your neighbors know that you'd like to institute a policy of not shouting over the dividers to each other—then stick to it!

Chair. Adjust your chair so you're in an upright position with lower back supported, knees equal with or slightly lower than hips, and feet flat. Use a footrest if your feet hang down—I found that a fourteen-inch piece of four-by-four lumber works perfectly. This will help maintain good posture, which is the maintenance of the normal curvature of your spine without undue pressure on joints and nerves. The benefits of good posture are instantaneous because you're preserving optimal organ, muscle, and joint function for energy and endurance. You also achieve greater concentration and mental ability when you eliminate the aching results of poor posture, not to mention promoting a more confident, vigorous appearance.

Computer. Your monitor should be approximately two to three inches above seated eye level. Twisting to see your screen adds to a feeling of tentativeness, so you'll gladly be distracted. Adjust your keyboard so that your shoulders are relaxed, elbows are in a slightly open position (100 to 110°), and wrists and hands are straight. Keep the mouse close to the keyboard. Train yourself to use it with your nondominant hand. This leaves your dominant hand free to type quickly and accurately, going back to the resting position on your keyboard. (Most keyboards have a little nub on the J and F keys to rest your index fingers on.)

Copy Stand. A document holder or copy stand right next to your monitor will keep you from leaning and twisting to see a document flat on your desk. It can be as simple as a stand-up clipboard or small note holder, or a more elaborate document holder that hangs off your monitor and tilts, has a line guide, magnifying lens, and a whiteboard.

Phone. If you are on the phone a lot throughout the day, it's a good idea to use a headset or speakerphone to eliminate cradling the handset. This makes talking on the phone less of a strain on your neck.

Lighting. The proper lighting in your office can reduce headaches and eyestrain. I realize that you don't have much control over this if you're in a cubicle, but often a swing-arm desk lamp will alleviate any shadows or darkness on your desk.

▶ Use natural light as much as possible by moving your desk near windows or under skylights.
▶ Reduce the glare and heat from windows with movable screens or adjustable blinds.
▶ Move equipment and computer monitor to eliminate glare.
▶ Use a swing-arm or clip-on lamp to illuminate tasks.

▶ Use a pole light facing upward or toward the wall to increase room brightness.

▶ Consider a full-spectrum light if you've got seasonal affective disorder.

Ventilation. Researchers at the Harvard School of Public Health found that office employees who work in areas that receive less fresh air from the outside are more likely to call in sick than their colleagues who breathe higher levels of outside air. This may result from the transmission of cold and flu viruses and other irritants that are not removed in ventilation systems with moderate airflow.

▶ Maintain air circulation, increasing with the number of people in the room.

▶ Open windows for fresh air from the outside whenever possible.

▶ Direct heating/air conditioning vents away from blowing on your face or head.

▶ Use a small desk fan or heater. Place it at your feet for maximum benefits. (Be careful that the heater isn't too close to furniture or combustibles and the fan doesn't disturb your papers.)

▶ Use saline nasal spray in dry months or with high temperatures—it will keep your nasal passages moist and less susceptible to floating irritants. Small humidifiers are great, and the cool-air types are easier on your nasal mucosa.

Coordinating Your Communications

At work, your communication style can be your greatest asset in reducing busyness. If ineffective, the way you manage your communications with others can cost you much time and cause many needless interruptions. In today's working world, face-to-face communication has taken a backseat to technology, making the way you handle e-mail and other online communication critical to your productivity. Fortunately, there are many smart, effective ways to maximize your use of e-mail, voice mail, and other technologies.

E-Mail and Your In(sane)-Box

In October 2008, the New York–based research firm Basex published a study of a thousand office workers from top managers on down. It found that interruptions (spam, unnecessary e-mail, and instant messaging) now consume an average of 2.1 hours each day, or 28 percent of the workday. The two hours of lost productivity included not only unimportant interruptions and distractions but also the recovery time associated with getting back on task. Researchers found workplace interruptions for those who perform tasks involving information cost the U.S. economy $617 billion a year (based on an average salary of $21 an hour for the 56 million knowledge workers). That is entirely too much productivity lost, hours that our economy could definitely use. Fortunately enough, this is a problem that can be solved on the individual level, and the solution begins with you! Here are some ideas for coordinating your office communications for maximum efficiency.

Lose the Noise. Turn off the alert sound. Not being able to hear it every time an e-mail comes your way will help wean you off your addiction to checking e-mail and immediately responding to or forwarding them.

Incoming E-Mails. Limit the number of times per day you check e-mail. When you're constantly reacting to every e-mail, your brain gets taken off the task at hand, and then it takes more time to get back on track. These constant distractions can add hours to your day and busyness. In *The 4-Hour Workweek*, author Timothy Ferriss advocates checking e-mail only twice a day, just before lunch and again at 4 P.M., but *never* first thing in the morning. If you decide to implement this strategy, make sure you let people know to expect it. Create an auto-response that states the times of day that you check and respond to e-mail. Make it friendly, and give your phone number as an option for urgent assistance.

Deprive Contact. Don't spoil your correspondents by responding too soon to e-mails, and stay off AOL Instant Messenger (AIM) or any version of instant messaging. Responding immediately or being always available can become a problem with how others perceive, and ultimately treat, you. It's a lot like dating—when someone's too available, they seem a little desperate and lose their mystery and value to you. The always-available date is nice and convenient at first, but your interest in your "easy date" lags sooner than if you have to work a little harder for his or her attention.

▶ **Filters.** Use the spam-filtering option on your e-mail software. Make filters for your boss, clients, coworkers, suppliers, friends, and family. I use a color-coding system, such as green for clients, red for priority, blue for friends, etc., and can quickly sort by color and attend to priorities without distractions.

▶ **Folders.** Make separate mailboxes or folders for current projects, cases, or clients. Keep it simple: the more folders you have, the less efficient it is to remember which folder goes with which project.

▶ **Establish rules.** Make agreements with coworkers to send only essential messages (i.e., eliminate "OK, thanks" notes) and to pick up the phone or meet in person only when a subject can be handled person-to-person better.

▶ **Forwards.** When it comes to e-mail forwards, there is a time and a place for everything, and it's rarely ever "at the office during work hours." I send a note to repeat offenders who constantly bombard me with those thought-you'd-like-this pieces: "I really appreciate your thinking of me, but please take me off your forward list." Being polite but firm about this gets the point across without hurting anyone's feelings. You could suggest instituting a no-forwarding policy in your office: no forwards unless absolutely necessary. This may be a delicate situation for many of you who are uncomfortable sending a "cease and desist" e-mail to your mother-in-law or elderly grandmother. You can tell your mimaw that it's your office policy or use the filtering system to direct e-mail from her and your other well-meaning forwarders to a special folder. (I don't recommend having two e-mail addresses because the point is to streamline messages.)

▶ **Declare bankruptcy.** As a last resort (and I mean *last*), if your in-box has hundreds of unanswered messages, you need to get a fresh start. Transfer all the unread messages to a new mailbox named "BK in-box." Don't read any of the messages. Instead, send a note to the senders of these e-mails that you can't respond: "I've gotten behind in my e-mail correspondence, and so I will have to get back to you later. If you still need my attention on this matter, please respond to this e-mail." Many times the problem has been solved already. If anyone answers this e-mail, you can start over with prioritizing your time and attention appropriate to the request. Warning: before you click "send" on your bankruptcy e-mail, make sure a message from your supervisor or boss is not in this batch.

Breaking your e-mail addiction is like breaking any other addiction: take it one day at a time. It's difficult, I know. Responding to e-mail is a fine way to get things done when your brain's too tired to do more demanding work, but the trick is to not let it take over your entire day.

Outgoing E-Mail

Getting a handle on your in(sane)-box, practicing anti-instant messaging, and following some basic guidelines on your outgoing e-mail can be big steps to bringing peace to your busyness at work and home.

▶ **Practice what you preach.** When sending e-mail to others, keep it simple, essential, and valuable. If you don't like receiving forwards (and if you want to de-busify, you probably shouldn't), don't forward e-mail to long lists of friends. If you must send mass e-mails, make them useful or meaningful. For example, you need to get out important information to all members of a project, need to update a group on a colleague's illness or tragedy, your contact info has changed, or you want to provide a URL for a website with a FAQ (frequently asked questions) section.

▶ **Subject line.** These should always precisely explain the reason for the message. "Meeting on Thursday morning changed" or "We can make the appointment" are great examples. Watch out for too many "Re: Re: Re:" pileups. These can bounce your e-mail into an intended recipient's spam folder or make you look lazy.

▶ **Humor.** Be careful with attempts at humor in your e-mails. Sarcasm works best in oral form. Writing a sarcastic message, you risk the reader taking it literally and considering what you said to be an outright nasty remark. Everyone's humor is specific, and you never know when you'll touch a nerve.

▶ **Politics.** See humor.

▶ **Cut emoticons.** Those cute little symbols showing emotions don't work. Instead, write what you mean: "I'm happy that," "It saddens me that," "I'm confused," "Please help me understand," "I like that you," "I'm disappointed," etc. Save the emoticons for text messaging with your kids. :-)

Telephone Tactics

How many times have you been cut off while leaving a voice-mail message? It's technology's way of telling you to "get to the point." Whether or not that seems rude, the quick cutoff ensures that callers will eventually learn to leave brief, informative messages. Don't wait until you get cut off before learning to keep it simple!

Tighten Your Message. Jot down a few drafts on scratch paper to keep you focused. More executives these days are only returning calls, not accepting them. Often your only hope of talking in person is to leave a compelling message. "I need to get your opinion on . . . ," "Can you make the session?" and "Please send me the contract" are all good examples of succinct messages.

Make a Script. Craft it, don't wing it. If you're going to be saying the same thing over and over on a sales call or a similar endeavor, writing a script will keep you fresh and on track. As you leave more messages, the script will naturally evolve until you have the perfect version locked down. At my therapeutic horseback riding center, we have volunteer calling parties to contact donors just to say, "thank you, we appreciate your support." We know that we'll mostly reach voice mail, so we craft our own script. Even if we happen to reach a real person, the script helps us stay on point—that this is purely an appreciation call, not a solicitation. In no time we've got a rockin' rhythm, and less than an hour later, a handful of us can leave hundreds of "you're great, and we love you" messages.

Ask Permission. This is just a matter of plain old good manners. When you get a human on the phone, ask, "Is this a good time?" They will usually tell you, then you can be assured of their attention or get a dedicated appointment later. Either way, it's a more civil way to initiate a conversation that may go a few minutes, and people like you to acknowledge that their time is valuable. Don't you?

Set Time Limits. When you receive a call, get the agenda up front. After the opening pleasantries, ask callers what you can do for them. They'll get to the point, and you can respond right away or reschedule the call. Not only will you save yourself time by doing this, but you will save callers time too (whether they realize this or not), and they just might appreciate it.

Quiet Times. If you're working on a project that needs focus, turn off your ringer—just like you should be doing with your e-mail alert! After a while, you'll be able to relax more knowing that you won't be interrupted, and you'll start instantly getting more done.

Work Habits That Work Wonders

If the word "deadline" causes you to go into overdrive and the thought of prioritizing tasks makes you wonder where to begin, read on. It's easier than you think. Following are tried-and-true everyday work habits that will increase your work confidence and decrease your busyness.

Integrate a Master List into Your Day Planner

Make a list of every project or important client you're working on right now—long-term and short-term. Use simple statements: "new marketing plan," "close ABC transaction," "make partner," "remodel storage area." Keep this on your desk so you can be brought back to the big picture anytime your busyness threatens to spin out of control. This is your master to-do list.

Keep with you a notebook or daily planner that holds your master list, broken down into yearly/monthly/daily goals to accomplish and frequently used phone numbers. Put goals and to-dos on small sticky notes. Pare down your "have-to-dos" each day. It's easy to move the notes around as your priorities change. Without dozens of loose notes floating around, you'll feel less hassled when the unexpected event eats up your day.

Plan Tomorrow Today

Before you leave work each day, refer to your master list and plan the most important tasks for the next day. Make notes of the things you did today—your accomplishments, large and small—right on your day planner or put a check by the tasks you accomplished. Move your sticky notes with goals and to-dos around on your day planner and arrange tasks in order of priority.

Power Through to the Finish

Carving out a continuous chunk of time to finish a project goes a long way toward reducing your stress. The time you save and the quality of the work you do when you power through to the finish far exceed any perceived benefits of continuous multitasking. You need to clearly establish a way to let people know that you can't be disturbed when you're in "the zone," especially if you work at home and family members tend to pop in and out: a sign on the door, wearing your lucky ball cap, a toy pit bull on the floor, etc.

- ▶ Make an appointment with yourself, just like any other important meeting, and go into hiding.
- ▶ Put on a headset or earbuds and play "thinking" music. The best for thinking is sixty beats per minute, no talking, such as Pachelbel's Canon in D. (I like Italian arias since they are soothing and my mind doesn't sing along.)
- ▶ Power through the project, and celebrate when you're done.

Don't Get Caught in the Web

Many employers will limit or prohibit online connection to the Internet except as it applies to performing your job. If you have unlimited access to the Web, you've probably discovered that you can lose hours if you don't control your online time. For me, it's easy to go from writing about stress reduction to researching psychoneuroimmunology articles to bidding on a new gizmo on eBay. Then I remember that I should put the old gizmo up for auction, organize the drawer it's in, take a digital picture of it, download my vacation pictures off the camera, and . . . wow, it's time for my conference call already! Set new rules for yourself online to stay task-oriented:

- ▶ Set alarms for when you must get *offline.*
- ▶ Use time-limiting or parental control software.

- Stay out of chat rooms.
- Shop only during lunch.
- Stay out of gaming sites.
- Visit social networking sites only during lunch.

Limit Interruptions

People popping into your office for a quick chat or snatching jelly beans from your candy bowl can be a pleasant break in the day. If you're working on a project that needs focus, interruptions can break your concentration so completely that their effects have been compared to drinking alcohol on the job! Despite all implications to the contrary, you do have the power to limit interruptions. Here's how:

- Eliminate visitation starters, such as snacks and funny signs.
- Keep your door closed more often.
- Hang a "Do Not Disturb" sign on your cubicle when you're in deep concentration.
- Talk to your coworkers about instituting "peace hours," time periods when no one interrupts anyone else in the office.

Practice Refusism

This may be the most difficult for you lovable, social types to institute at work. Whenever possible, get in the habit of saying no. Of course, you won't always be able to say no to the tasks you are asked to perform (unless your goal is to get fired), but if you find that you're easily pushed into taking on unnecessary work, then it's time to start using *no* more. You may think that you don't know how to do this, but when you were a two-year-old, *no* was probably your favorite word.

Here's a semi-radical exercise for you people pleasers out there. For one entire day, practice saying no to every request that doesn't come directly from your supervisor. Keep a journal to record how many times you said it and estimate how much time and effort you saved yourself. You will be surprised by how much time you saved by saying no. This provides positive reinforcement, which will make it easier to say no next time. Also, record the negative consequences of saying no—you might be surprised that there are very few!

Schedule Regular Tasks

It's easy with software like Microsoft Outlook, or your trusty paper scheduling system, to automate those things that happen all the time. You think you'll remember these "regular" events, but the basics can "fall through the cracks" when you're ultra-busy.

▶ **Vacations and days off.** Downtime is mandatory for rehabilitating your "busy."
▶ **Important birthdays and anniversaries.** Make sure to also note the year of the first one so you can be the one to acknowledge milestones: "Congrats on your 10th," or "Can you believe it's been three years?!" This kind of personal attention helps you distinguish yourself among your peers as a conscientious and caring person.
▶ **Bill-paying dates.** Put a "Bills" reminder on the first and fifteenth of each month, "Taxes" when quarterlies or property taxes are due. You'd be surprised how easy it is to miss a *monthly* or *yearly* deadline when you're busy. This system can be used for bills at your office and your own bills at home. Entrepreneurs find it easier to do both home and office bills at the same

time since they're on the system and have their "bill-paying rhythm" going.

▶ **Project deadlines.** Don't skip or overlook a vital step toward the finale. Keep yourself on track with automated deadlines every step of the way, depending on the demands of the project.

Time-Saving Tips

When talking about the biggest work time wasters, my clients invariably bring up two subjects: "trade" or professional reading and dreaded meetings. Both of these can be invaluable; professional reading keeps us current in our fields, and meetings, well, we can't do without them. Read on for strategies that will help you to keep these from becoming (1) a stack of dusty periodicals that has taken over a corner—or most—of your office and (2) an endless series of aimless, never-ending excuses for eating doughnuts with your coworkers.

Reduce Professional Reading

Is your professional reading piling up on the corner of your desk or sideboard? It's important to stay on top of what's going on in the industry, but somehow this priority is usually the first one to slip down to your "C-list." Instead of building a tower on your desk with your journals and magazines that will take up all kinds of space, use this method that I learned from the smartest businesswoman I know.

1. When you receive the magazine or journal, immediately go through the table of contents.
2. Mark whatever topics jump out at you.
3. Tear out the articles you marked.

4. Throw the rest of it in your recycle bin. (You do have one, don't you?)
5. Place the original articles in a folder marked "Waiting." Keep the folder in your briefcase, purse, or office bag.
6. Read whenever you have the opportunity—in a long line, waiting at the airport, or on telephone hold.
7. Toss it right then if you're not going to keep it.
8. If you're going to keep it, make notes on the upper right-hand corner by the title—(a) date you read it, (b) relevance to you, and (c) where it should be filed. For example, an article on updated tax law would be put in your "Taxes" folder.
9. Empty the "Waiting" file once a month. If you haven't digested the information by then, you probably don't need it, or it's out of date.

Hold Meetings with TALENT

People who have attended my workshops have cited meetings as their biggest time and energy waster. Often there is no better way to disseminate information, get people's buy-in, keep them excited about a project, build consensus, or just to make things happen. In order that your meetings don't turn into "death by PowerPoint" or just another time to text friends under the table, show off your TALENT.

T Setting a **time limit** shows that you value everyone's time.

A Have an **agenda** and stick to it. This will give you ammunition for complainers and power players.

L **Lead** whenever possible. Show some authority, and you'll stand out.

E No **extra** people: never invite people who don't belong, because they will surely pull you off track.

N **Never** meet unnecessarily. Do you really need one *every* Thursday?

T **Timely** follow-up ensures that you'll get people to keep commitments. They know you'll be checking. This is a good time to praise them.

To Clone or Not to Clone

The goal of all these new office initiatives is not to make you a drone clone but to help with your "busy." I promise that you'll still be able to be *you*—hold onto your personality and be friendly at work—especially after these tips and skills turn you into a higher functioning, less frantic worker. Many "work smarter" strategies can be uncomfortable at first, but you'll soon wonder why you ever did it any other way. Ultimately, when you're working smarter, you'll be taking care of yourself, managing your busyness, and bringing civility back to your workplace.

Chapter 6

Getting De-Stressed at Work

When we are unable to find tranquility within ourselves, it is useless to seek it elsewhere.

—François de La Rochefoucauld

When you're in a high-stress position at work, that just means you have to work equally hard at decreasing your stress. The most obvious way to do so is by taking more time for hobbies and relaxation outside of work. If only it were that easy, right? But unfortunately, you can't simply devote more time to decompressing with outside hobbies right now because . . .

- Your job demands you be the first one in and last one out.
- You seem to do others' jobs to make sure they're done right.
- Every task you take on eventually leaves you ultra-busy.
- You see no end in sight for your current task.
- You've begun to feel anxious or guilty when not doing work.

What follows are quick tips, essential skills, and simple exercises for you to get relief from stress while you're still at work. While you might not always be able to de-stress by leaving the office, you can do so while you're still there. You will not only lower your own stress, but you might just bring more hope, levity, and optimism to your workplace.

Get Relief Now

You're busy and stressed. Who has time for a mind-cleansing run or a twenty-minute soak in the tub? What you need is relief right now. That's where these exercises come in. They are like a pressure-relief valve for when your stress levels begin to climb a little too high. They won't solve any of the big problems in your life, but they will ease a bit of the tension that you may be going through at work on any given day.

Belly Breathing

Did you know that you can switch off the stressed part of your nervous system just by paying close attention to your breathing? Your fight-or-flight response kicks in whenever you are anxious or stressed. This triggers your breathing to become quicker and shallower by moving your breathing from your belly to your chest. At the same time, your stress hormones suppress the flow of chemicals that have a calming effect.

When you take a deep breath, don't just inhale and blow it out fast. Correct breathing involves the entire torso, especially the abdominal wall muscles. Your chest should expand in all directions, your tongue should rest lightly on the gums behind your front teeth, and your jaw should be slack. This can be done sitting at your desk. Allow your hands to rest on your lower belly and to rise and fall with each breath. This should come naturally, but often it doesn't. You'll figure it out in no time and be on your way to a stress-free moment.

Four-Square Breathing

Here is another breathing exercise you can do, only this one involves some visualization. Close your eyes and picture a square. Then try to imagine traveling along one side of this square while you inhale and count to four. When you reach the corner of the square, hold your breath and count to four. Then exhale while traveling along the next side, hold your breath, and count to four. Continue this pattern until you're back where you started. This simple exercise will give your mind a much-needed break.

A Quick Thump

The thymus is an organ located in the upper anterior portion of the chest cavity just behind the breastbone, beneath the hollow of the throat. This organ produces cells important to your immune system, which is often taxed during periods of high stress. Since the thymus gland's activity slows as we age, it makes sense to keep it stimulated in times of stress.

Use your fingertips, alternating with the right and left hand, to deliver a tap (or thump) on your sternum for about twenty thumps. Easy does it, though, you're not trying to restart your heart, just stimulate your thymus. You can learn to calm yourself in particularly stressful situations by using this technique.

On the Rack

Do some stretches like you're on one of those medieval racks. Stand up, slowly reach your fingertips to the ceiling, and stretch higher as you yawn deeply. While sitting, stretch your legs straight out from your hips, reach forward pointing your toes, and then slowly point them toward the

ceiling (good to do undetected while sitting at the conference table).

Go to Your Place

Where is the most peaceful place on earth to you? Is it your
favorite fishing hole, a place you visited on vacation, or
somewhere you hope to see in the near future? Sit back and
picture yourself there right now. Imagine what you're looking at, who is there with you, the weather, the sounds, the
smells. Consider it a little mental vacation to get away from
all the stress associated with being at work.

Check Your "Duh" Factors

In some instances, it's abundantly clear just what the problem is. You can point to one person, situation, or activity
and label it definitively as the reason you need to de-stress.
Other times, being stressed starts with a series of small
insults to your body and soul that eventually take a major
toll on your overall well-being. Let's take a look at some of
the obvious-to-everyone-but-you causes of stress, the "duh"
factors—those things that slowly erode your comfort when
you really ought to know better.

Your Clothes

Are they too tight? The wrong length? Do they pinch you
across the shoulders? Are the armholes strangling your
arms? Do you wear control-top *anything*? If it's not comfortable, it has got to go, because discomfort equals stress. Years
ago I realized that I was uncomfortable wearing skirts, so
I replaced them with slacks. This simplified my life, especially while traveling, and I'm more comfortable being my
true-to-self tomboy.

Your Shoes

You will rarely hear a man say that his shoes are killing him. Are your shoes too tight, too high, or uncomfortable for *any* reason? Get rid of them or keep a comfy pair beneath your desk. I had to get used to "my look" being in flats rather than heels. It took a while to sink in, but it was worth it for the comfort. Besides, now I can sprint through an airport with the best of them.

Your Posture

Your mother was right—you *do* need to sit up straight, young lady! Your stress may be aided and abetted by poor posture, which can lead to tight, aggravated muscles and connective tissues around the spine. Do body-checks throughout the day, focusing on sitting and standing straighter than normal. While standing, your ears, shoulders, hips, and heels should be lined up perpendicular to the ground. If you are sitting in a chair, your ears should stack up over your shoulders and hips. The best posture is when your back feels weightless and long and your head feels light on your shoulders.

Your Frown

For some people, a frown is their face's natural default setting. Are you one of them? You'll know the answer by the time the permanent lines etch themselves in your face. In the meantime, smile for no apparent reason and smile often. The mood that tends to accompany frowning will be counteracted, and you'll even be sending a message to your brain to release some of those great natural drugs that relax your body.

Your Eating and Snacking

Many of us snack unconsciously or by routine. We have the emergency candy bar in our desk drawer or grab a cup of coffee out of habit. Caffeine, energy drinks, and sweet snacks can yo-yo your blood sugar, stressing you more as your mood and energy level fluctuate. Replace the junk food with small packages of dry-roasted nuts and plain water. Keep your own water-filtering pitcher at your desk to control bottled water costs and litter.

A Positive Attitude Alleviates Stress

All the stretching and breathing in the world won't do much to reduce your stress if you don't do a mental tune-up also. Changing your attitude can change your perception of your job, thereby lowering your stress. Remember, it's usually your perception of the event that causes you stress, not the event itself. Here are some simple attitude adjustments you can make to adjust your stress response.

Be Ready to Laugh

Occasionally we get so caught up in the drudgery of working that we completely lose our sense of humor. But if you take everything too seriously, you're setting yourself up for stress. Laughter *is* the best medicine. Next time you find yourself in a funk, laugh your way out of it! My best friend and mentor, Lola Gillebaard, has honed humor to a fine point. (She was a finalist for the reality TV show "Last Comic Standing.") Having a funny pal like her helps anytime I need a quick jolt of humor in my day. Being around her has also taught me to look for the light side of a problem. This helps to lighten the tone of almost any office crisis.

Sound Like a Happy Person

If you use the phone a lot on the job, place a small mirror where you can check your expression. By smiling as you answer your phone, you have a better chance of affecting a positive outcome in your conversation. Adopting a happy tone in face-to-face interactions can reduce stress on both sides. This is not just good business policy or customer service; it's good brain maintenance. As with a big goofy smile (genuine or not), you can actually change your own brain chemistry for the better when you sound happier. And happy people tend to be some of the least stressed-out folks among us.

Curb Your Complaining

Sometimes our reactions to a stressful situation can alienate other people. This in turn creates more stress from having to face the situation alone. A good way to keep others from wanting to help you is to have the dark cloud hanging over you that results from whining and complaining.

Check these behaviors at the door in a time of stress, and you'll get more help when you ask for it. I know that it's sometimes stress relieving to have a good old-fashioned gripe session, but the less you do it at work, the more people will want to be around you.

Park Your Perfectionism

As a recovered perfectionist I (gradually) learned that this condition comes from an all-or-nothing mentality. I had a tendency to decide that if something I was working on was not perfect, it was garbage. During this period of my life, if one part of a project went wrong, I considered the whole thing totally messed up. This is just way too much pressure to put on oneself. The drive for perfection is one of the surest ways to get stressed-out. Shoot for optimum instead of perfect and you'll feel much better.

Anchor Your Anger

Everyone gets worked up over things. Anger, in and of itself, isn't bad. What's damaging is anger as a lifestyle. Duke University published a study indicating that people who are chronically angry have four to seven times the risk of terminal heart disease and cancer as those not prone to anger. Researchers believe that hostility is the personality trait most useful in predicting heart disease. What is even more surprising is that the "silent seethers" are at greater risk than the "blow up" types.

The next time you feel the anger coming on, ask yourself the following questions:

▶ Is this really so important? (Is it a deal breaker, life or death?)
▶ Am I justified in my anger? (Really?)
▶ Can I do anything to deal with the situation?

A "no" to any one of these questions signals you to calm yourself down. Research bears out that if the situation isn't really important, anger only adds to your stress. Also, if you can't reasonably defend your anger or do anything about the situation, your anger is hurting you more than anyone else—even threatening your health.

Release Your Resentment

Holding a grudge is one sure way to up your stress at work. Has somebody done you wrong? It's critical that you figure out some way to let go of your resentment. Your body actually relives a bad experience every time you think of it. Recently, I was given the opportunity to participate in a very significant (and lucrative) series of speaking engagements. It was determined that I would share this chance with three other women. When the client sent the calendar to the first woman, she convinced them to give her *90 percent* of the speeches. I was stunned, then angry, then livid. It was all I could think about—and whine about—to my husband and close friends. Things like, "How could she? The dog. She'll get hers some day." Nice, eh?

Shortly after I swallowed this gut-bomb, I attended a lecture of one of my favorite spiritual leaders. I didn't know his topic until I got there: how to *let go of things*. "Oh my gosh," I thought, "how did he know?" One exercise had us writing our disappointments, angers, and frustrations on a piece of paper. We skewered this paper with a long nail and swirled it in a solution, saying, "It is gone." The paper totally dissolved! I'll never forget my little-kid glee at seeing the paper be *gone* like magic.

I actually did begin to feel better when I thought of the situation and the dissolving paper. My dear friend Lola would say, "Gone" every time I started. Eventually, my anger faded, and I saw the gift in the incident: the time commitment involved in taking on that project would have prevented me from other opportunities (namely delivering this book on time!).

Let It Roll Off Your Back

Do you have someone who thinks you can't do anything right or is quick to point out your flaws? Learning to keep harmony *in* yourself and *between* yourself and others will ease stress in the workplace. Practice these steps:

1. Absorb the harsh comment or criticism.
2. Halt the urge to respond quickly or defend your position.
3. Say, "I appreciate your comments," while nodding slowly.
4. Don't say anything else.
5. Repeat as necessary.

It's amazing how often these comments or criticisms are made just to get a reaction out of you. By denying the perpetrator the pleasure of your angry response, and even acknowledging the suggestion, you gain the edge that comes with remaining cool and not rising to the bait.

Learn to Call Time-Out

In nearly every sport, a coach can call time-out, usually to realign a strategy or because a player is injured. When you're feeling strategically weak or injured, ask for time out by saying, "I'd like to give this some thought. Let's pick up our discussion tomorrow morning at ten." This helps you examine how the matter fits into your master plan. When asked to change your plan, you'll keep your stress down if you allow for time to examine the options.

Employ Silence

Most of us tend to respond *immediately* based on our perspective. Try *not* responding—well, not responding vocally anyway. I once had a mentor who could raise one eyebrow without another facial movement. It said so much with so little. Just her single raised eyebrow allowed her to keep her cool when faced with an irate customer. Eventually, her silence allowed the person to vent, cool down, and then grant her a chance to actually solve the problem. Remember, less can often be more. The next time you feel an urge to respond immediately with words . . . take a deep breath, let it out slowly, look thoughtful, and see what happens next.

Be a Better Listener

Before you yield to the urge to add your two cents to a conversation, stop! Ask yourself, "What are they saying to me—through their voice and body language?" Do you assume you know before you allow them to finish? Note the following about the speaker:

▶ **Body position.** An open stance (arms relaxed, legs uncrossed) signals willingness to cooperate, whereas a closed posture (arms folded, legs crossed, body turned away) indicates a strong negative feeling and difficulty to persuade.

▶ **Vocal tone and volume.** Higher and louder indicates heightened emotion.

▶ **Facial expression.** One's face shows the universal emotions of joy, sadness, anger, fear, contempt, and disgust.

▶ **Gestures.** Arms waving can indicate excitement, hands clenched means anger, and finger-pointing can convey dominance.

Before you speak, decide if what someone is saying is a complaint, observation, opinion, gossip, or just chatter. Respond accordingly. Sometimes just being able to gauge what someone is communicating to you through body language can ease the stress that comes with incorrectly pegging someone's state of mind. Pay close attention to what is being said without words.

Save Yourself Stress in the Long Run

Looking back on situations that have caused you trouble, how often have you said "I would'a gone about it differently if I only knew what she really wanted," "I could'a done it on time if I'd only asked him to help me," or "I should'a never brought up our history." Use these wise strategies when dealing with people so that you'll have less would'a, could'a, should'a and stress in your life.

Ask Questions First

A great way to appear capable and in control is by taking on new tasks and projects with a calm nod and cool demeanor. Unfortunately, playing the role of superstar at the office seems to require that you already know how to do everything. That is not the case at all. Give yourself a break—*of course* you don't already know how to do everything! You will only add to your stress by wondering where to start and trying to figure out how you'll ever get it done. Before you project an air of the countess of control, question

- What your obligations are, specifically
- What the expected time line is
- Who else should be included or excluded
- What topics or areas should be avoided
- What has been tried already
- What materials you will need
- Anything at all that is unclear (better to find out sooner rather than later)

Delegate

I know, I know, "If it's going to be done right, I need to do it myself." In some instances, though, this attitude can be really unhealthy. When you have a big project, it's better to decide what only you can do and where your strengths will be best put to use, and then assign the other tasks to somebody else. You *can't* treat every aspect of every project as a high priority that only you can take on—you end up doing a mediocre job that way. If the project suffers because you did everything on your own and rushed it out, you might also stress over how you could have done better—if you only had the time. That is exactly what delegating does: it saves you time so you can get the job done right. As an added bonus, delegating shows that you have faith in your coworkers, which leads to higher morale around the office and a less stressful atmosphere all around.

Know When to Go with Your Gut

Use your common sense and simple solutions by trusting your gut instincts more. Be wary of fancy solutions when a simple, from-the-gut strategy will do. Lee Iacocca turned around an ailing Chrysler Corporation by tapping into his own experience with what worked and listening to his gut when making decisions. You haven't made it this far in life by weighing and pondering each and every decision. Try making more quick decisions based on the information you have at the time. You won't always be right, but you'll save yourself the stress of worrying over every detail. You might be surprised how often you *do* get it right when you learn to trust your instincts.

Pick Your Battles Wisely

When I was in college, we marched and protested just about everything and anything; giving equal weight to the large and small causes. An end to war and a demand for colder milk in the cafeteria were both argued for with intensity because, being young and idealistic, everything was a battle.

After you've been in the work world, though, you realize that fighting for everything you believe in takes more energy and time than it's worth. Sometimes being right just isn't worth the stress it takes to get there. Choose your battles wisely and don't waste your time and energy on things that are out of your control. The next time you are in a situation the outcome of which you want to influence, ask yourself the following questions:

▶ What camp is this going to put me into? (complainers, etc.)
▶ Will this serve me well?
▶ Is it possible?
▶ What are realistic chances of success?

Dive into It Now!

Get started on that project or task as soon as possible. The sooner you start, the more time you will have to let your brilliance percolate. You'll also see potential roadblocks in time to do something about them. If it's a report, do a brain dump (BD)—a first draft—and put it away in a file. (Be sure to save it and back up.) When you read the BD later, your creativity will naturally take over. When you aren't burdened with the immediacy of being up against a deadline, you tend to come up with ideas and examples that remain elusive during a caffeine-induced all-nighter. Procrastination only creates more stress, whereas the multistep process lowers your stress and actually makes the end product better. (Believe me, you wouldn't want to read my BD on this chapter!)

Silly Desk Yoga

All of the advice in this chapter can help you avoid a lot of unnecessary stress in your life. Some degree of stress is inevitable, though—especially at the office. And that, my friends, is why you need to learn how to perform "silly desk yoga," the latest way to soothe jangled nerves and loosen up stressed muscles. These simple yoga stretches, exercises, and tips offer you an opportunity to make your working hours more productive, your body healthier, and your mind revitalized.

You can use silly desk yoga whenever you're by yourself—at your desk during a conference call, teleseminar, or webinar, or when you're trapped in a traffic jam. A lot of times throughout the day, there is little else you can do but sit there, so why not use the time to refresh yourself?

A very important part of my transformation into a recovered control freak involved learning how to relax with simple yoga techniques. I've put together this collection of exercises and tips so you too can learn how to get instant relaxation. You don't have to buy into a complete makeover of your psyche or commit to hours at the gym or yoga studio. All you need is the desire to loosen the tightness in your neck, back, and shoulders or to avoid having to bite your tongue at a meeting or in a traffic jam.

Get Ready to Get Silly

These movements come from many diverse relaxation and exercise experiences—stretching, Pilates, yoga, and therapeutic horseback riding. They weren't designed for you to look cool or like an exercise expert. In fact, some of the movements are downright goofy looking, but *they work*!

Yes, you'll feel strange while making funny faces at your desk, but *they work*! Your coworkers might whisper that you're getting weird(er), but you *will* be less stressed.

Warning: Don't do any exercises that cause you pain. If you are currently under medical care, check with your health-care provider before doing these movements.

Before You Get Started—Do the "Head Check"

It is important that you do the "Head Check" before you begin your silly desk yoga movements. It provides you with an opportunity to experience the difference in your body, and this will support your muscle memory. The more you use the Head Check, the more aware you'll be of how well the movements are working for you. All these exercises and movements are best when done in the following order shown. They should be done slowly and smoothly—don't rush, jerk, or sweat it. Begin by sitting balanced with your back in a relaxed-but-straight position, both your feet flat on the floor.

The Head Check for your current range of motion of your head, neck, and shoulders follows:

1. Sit straight in a chair with your hands on your thighs and both feet flat on the floor.
2. Keeping your head level, turn it *slowly* and *smoothly* in one direction. Keep your chin parallel to the ground and avoid rotating your head diagonally backwards. Turn only as far as you can comfortably without force or strain.
3. Notice how far behind your shoulder you can see. Mark the farthest place you can spot on the wall. These markers will be referred to as your "spots."

4. Return your head slowly to the starting point and repeat to the other side. (One side is usually "tighter" than the other.)

5. Hold three fingers (index, middle, ring) like the "Scout salute" and insert them gently into your mouth (wash hands first, please).

6. Note the tightness in your jaw and the ease—or lack thereof—of inserting your finger.

Remember your spots on the wall and the amount of tightness in your jaw. Your initial Head Check will be used as a reference point for later comparison.

Your Head and Jaw

Stress tends to manifest physically in certain areas of your body. For many people, the head and jaw are the main locations in which stress reveals itself. The slightest change in the comfort of your head and jaw will affect the rest of your body.

▶ **Jaw movements.**
Move your jaw *slowly* side to side eight to ten times and then jut your lower jaw forward and backward *slowly* eight to ten times. Be careful if you have temporomandibular joint (TMJ) problems. Do not grind your teeth; leave your jaw loose.

Jaw movements

▶ **Tongue movements.**
Stick your tongue *out*
and *down* to the right,
move it to the left, and
back again; repeat eight
to ten times. Stick your
tongue *out* and *up* to
the right, then move
it to the left and back
again; repeat eight to
ten times.

Tongue movements

Are you feeling silly yet?
Just wait!

▶ **Eye movements.** With
both eyes together, look
up and to the right,
then to the left and back
again; repeat eight to ten
times.

Now . . . you've *got to* be
starting to feel silly with the
next set!

Eye movements

▶ **Combo movements.** In opposition, move your
tongue down and to the right while both your eyes
look up and to the left. Then, move your tongue down
and to the left while both your eyes look up and to the
right. Repeat eight to ten times.

Combo movement A

Combo movement B

Switch by moving your tongue up and to the right while both your eyes look down and to the left. Then, move your tongue up and to the left while both your eyes look down and to the right. Repeat eight to ten times.

Now, do the Head Check again and note your "spots" and your jaw tension. Do you notice an improved range of motion? Not so silly, after all!

There is a simple explanation as to why these exercises work. You are moving the muscles and joints that tend to get locked when you are concentrating, on a tight deadline, or under normal stress. As well, you are breaking patterns of muscle memory and cross-firing the nerves to break these blockages.

Your Head and Neck

After doing the previous movements, move on to the following exercises that are designed to release stress and tightness in your neck and increase your flexibility. Since muscles, tendons, and ligaments supporting your head on the top of your spine are many and complex, it takes very little stress for them to cause you discomfort.

▶ **Head shaking.** Stay seated or standing comfortably, looking straight ahead with your arms hanging relaxed at your sides. Shake or "jiggle" your head side to side in small one-inch movements. Try to use very little effort and continue being relaxed in your head and neck. Continue this motion for thirty to sixty seconds.

   Move your head slightly to the left (about 30 degrees) and jiggle your head for thirty to sixty seconds. Repeat with your starting position 30 degrees to the right of center.

▶ **Massaging the occipital joint.** Use your index, middle, and ring fingers of both hands to massage the area between your skull and first neck vertebra (the occipital joint). Softly and gently, continue in a circular motion for thirty to sixty seconds.

   Leave the fingers on the joint, *stop* massaging, and stretch your elbows out to the side as much as you can comfortably. At the same time gently move your head forward 25 to 30 degrees; hold ten seconds. Return your head back to neutral, then gently move your head backward 25 to 30 degrees; hold ten seconds. Repeat two to three times.

▶ **Skull massage.** Use two fingers to firmly massage the base of your skull (the bumps behind your earlobes). Vary the method from up/down to front/back, in small circles. Continue thirty to sixty seconds, then switch to your other side. At first, this may be uncomfortable, but this will lessen when the massage is done several times a day.

▶ **Jaw massage.** Use three fingers to lightly massage your jaw "hinge." Use small circles forward and backward, varying the speed and intensity. (Again, be careful if you have TMJ problems.) Continue thirty to sixty seconds and finish by using your flattened hand to press firmly (without movement) for ten to fifteen seconds. Release, smile.

▶ **Neck tilts.** Neck tilts should not create pain, so remember to move gently and slowly. Inhale, and stretch your spine upward through the top of your head. Keep your sternum (breastbone) lifted. On exhale, allow your head to tilt toward your left shoulder. Hold, and relax for several breaths. Repeat on the other side. Don't allow your back to round as you breathe while in this position.

Now, do the Head Check and note your spots. What is the improvement in your range of motion?

Your Shoulders and Upper Torso

To relax your shoulders and upper torso, you need to "perfect the pluck." A pluck uses your thumb and your index and middle fingers in a quick pinching motion.

▶ **Shoulder plucking.** Using your left hand on your right shoulder, pinch the large muscle that runs between your neck and shoulder, the trapezius. Pluck the "cord" up and away, then repeat twice. Switch hands/sides. This is a quick motion. This exercise may feel tender at first but will get to be more comfortable as the muscle relaxes. You can also do this lying in bed when you first wake up.

▶ **Finger fan.** With your shoulders and neck relaxed, reach your hands forward at shoulder height and width, keeping your wrists straight. Spread your fingers wide, hold five seconds, and relax. Repeat four to six times.

Your Back and Spine

Your *starting position* is sitting on the front part of a chair, placing your hands on your thighs and your feet flat on the ground and shoulder width apart. Your body will form four right angles: chin to torso, torso to thigh, thigh to calf, calf to foot.

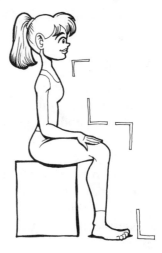

The starting position

Warning: Don't do any exercises that cause you pain. *Never* drop your head forward of backward fast or heavily. If you are currently under medical care, check with your health-care provider before doing these movements.

The Spine Check for the current range of motion of your back and spine follows:

1. In the starting position, *gently and without force*, lift your head and eyes toward the ceiling.
2. Note "your spot."
3. How far up the ceiling can you see easily?

Remember your spot on the ceiling. Your initial Spine Check will be used as a reference point for later comparison and your starting position (as in the figure) should be maintained for all the following exercises.

▶ **Back arch.** In the starting position, slowly lift your head and eyes toward the ceiling while arching your back gently. Slowly return to starting position. Repeat three to five times.

▶ **Rounded back.** In the starting position, slowly rotate your head and eyes so they face the ground while rounding your back at the same time. Try to imagine wrapping yourself around a basketball. Slowly return to the starting position. Repeat three to five times.

▶ **Knee pull.** In the starting position, lift your right knee toward your chest by placing your left hand under the knee and wrapping your right hand around your kneecap. Gently and slowly pull your knee to the point that you feel a *very slight* stretch in your lower back. Hold this position for ten seconds. Gently put your knee down and switch legs. Do three to five repetitions on each side.

▶ **Seated toe stretch.** In the starting position, lift the toes of both feet up and down simultaneously and then lift the toes of each foot alternately. Play with speed and rhythm.

▶ **Seated heel lift.** Do the same by lifting your heels—up and down together, then alternately up and down. Play with speed and rhythm.

▶ **Seated toe circles.** Maintain your starting position; lift your right heel up. Circle your toes clockwise slowly ten times, then counterclockwise ten times. Repeat on your left side.

▶ **Seated heel circles.** Maintain your starting position; lift your right toes up. Circle your heel clockwise slowly ten times, then counterclockwise ten times. Repeat on your left side.

Your Grand Finale

Congratulations! You have just completed your first session of silly desk yoga. Now is the time for the final tests to prove that you *really are* looser, more relaxed, and less stressed.

1. Do the Head Check for your range of motion for your head, neck, and shoulders.
2. Note your spots. How much farther can you move your head to the right and to the left?
3. Do the Spine Check for your range of motion of your back and spine.
4. Note your spot. How much farther can you see on the ceiling?

The Payoff

Of all the activities that make up your daily living, loosening up your head, neck, shoulders, and back are the ones that give you both immediate and long-term payoff. By reducing the tightness a little each day—or, better yet, several times a day—you'll be avoiding greater, more painful problems such as headaches, stiff neck, and back spasms. The beauty of using silly desk yoga is that your body will let you know when it is needed and how well you're managing.

Your Plan of Action

Why is it that some people can handle a stress-producing event or situation? And others blow up, masterfully avoid it, or internalize it by developing a variety of physical symptoms? It's all what *your* stress means to *you* and *what you do about it*. Right now, make a commitment to what you are going to do about stress at work. It's important to have a plan of action that will keep you on track for reducing your stress. Make a list for yourself that covers the following:

▶ The one action I will take this week is _____ .
▶ Within two weeks, I will _____ .
▶ Within one month, I will _____ .
▶ In six months I will handle my work stress this way: _____ .

Lowering your stress allows your body and mind to work more efficiently—making you less busy. Using these stress-relief methods and changing your attitude about your stressors, you'll be preventing future stress—and busyness.

Chapter 7

Dissecting Disharmony at Work

The meeting of two personalities
is like the contact of two chemical
substances: if there is any reaction,
both are transformed.

—C. G. Jung

What does dealing with difficult people have to do with your busyness? They take up a disproportionate amount of your time and sap your energy, and you will be around them for the rest of your life. If you start coping with them, you'll save time and energy in the long run. Even in small doses, difficult people have the same effect as water rushing over a stone. Over time the constant friction will eventually wear you down.

You've been allowing these jerks to take up your time, or you might even be trying to outlast them. After all, if they would just go away (move, quit, transfer), that problem would be solved. I've heard clients say, "I'm just going to hang in there *until* the children are out of school (the holidays, the weekend, I get my bonus)." *Until* is dangerous because little by little you are worn smooth by compliance with jerky behavior. Each infraction adds up so at the end of your day, year, or life, you have allowed someone else's bad behavior to triumph over your soul.

Do you sometimes feel like your job is perfect except for some of your clients, customers, or patients? Do you work with a few people who range from unpleasant to downright mean? I call the difficult people in my life "lions." Some of them may act like pussycats, but you need to think of them as lions. From a distance, lions and difficult people are impressive and charismatic, but up close, if you're not vigilant, they are stress-producing and can rip you apart.

When you decide to tame the lions in your life, the crazy busyness in your life can't help but improve. This chapter will show how you can take your life back and tame that person—or persons—who leaves you feeling frustrated, manipulated, or stressed. If your lion is a direct supervisor or an immediate coworker, Chapter 8 will help you broaden and fine-tune your skills when dealing with him or her.

You Need to COPE

You are not alone. Many studies have cited that most folks shut up, buckle down, and take it. In 2005, researchers Charlotte Rayner and Loraleigh Keashly reported that 25 percent of victims of bullies at work leave their jobs (compared to the average rate of 5 percent). The remaining 75 percent just stay and cope with it. It is noteworthy to mention that nasty people affect more than their intended target—in the same report, 20 percent of witnesses to bullying left their jobs.

Here is your big, grown-up, mature awakening: **you** are going to have to be the one who changes, because your *Devil Wears Prada* boss probably got (and keeps) his or her job by conducting him- or herself that way. They are not going to "see the light" no matter how clever, smart, or manipulative you are in trying to change them.

So your job is to COPE with difficult people.

C Find your own **character** and **craving**. Who are you, and what do you want to happen in this situation? (This saves you time and lowers your stress.)

O Stay **open** to alternatives to what you've done in the past.

P Make a **plan** and work it, based on knowledge and understanding of yourself.

E **Exit**, if necessary, the situation or the relationship.

Personal Teflon

Cecelia loves her job as a radio producer. She was living and working her dream as she was getting her master's degree in communications. She lives in her dream city, and the size of its radio market helps to confirm that she has "made it." She describes her coworkers as "high-energy, unfocused, artistic, and more than a little egomaniacal." At first she was impressed by some of these qualities, but now they drive her crazy. Basically Cecelia is even tempered and unruffled, but she realizes that if she wants to change the culture of "ultra-busy" at her station and lower her stress, it's up to her to make the first step.

I believe that one of the greatest inventions of the twentieth century is Teflon. In the kitchen, it allows you to cook with high heat, yet it makes cleanup easy. Oh sure, you can burn the baloney out of something, but it *won't stick*. When you discover your communication style, it's like your very own personal Teflon: when the heat's on, people's bad behaviors don't stick to you. It's a cleaner way to operate.

My students have found that in most interactions between people, the person who is most *self-aware* will be in command of the conversation—"If I know more about myself than you know about yourself, I will be in control of the conversation." Taking this knowledge further to include awareness of others will help you have great influence over their behavior—"If I know more about you than you know about *yourself*, I can control you."

Since you have spent your entire life developing your style and perfecting who you are, the following exercise will help you know more about you and your personal communication style. Later on in this chapter, you will discover how to know more about your lions and other difficult people.

Pick the following words that apply to *you* most of the time (i.e., "I am more lively than quiet."). Don't think too long about your answer—go with your first thought. Check one word from each pair.

Column A   **Column B**

☐ More lively	or	☐ more quiet
☐ More competitive	or	☐ more cooperative
☐ More extroverted	or	☐ more introverted
☐ More exacting	or	☐ more tolerant
☐ More of a doer	or	☐ more of a thinker
☐ More cheerful	or	☐ more serious
☐ More challenging	or	☐ more lenient
☐ More confronting	or	☐ more compromising
☐ More talkative	or	☐ more reserved
☐ More liberal	or	☐ more conservative
☐ More flashy	or	☐ more reserved
☐ More concerned	or	☐ more restrained
☐ More eager	or	☐ more meek

☐ More insistent	or	☐ more easygoing
☐ More outspoken	or	☐ more understated

Column B total _____

Column C   ## Column D

☐ More theatrical	or	☐ more conforming
☐ More impromptu	or	☐ more planned
☐ More instinctive	or	☐ more deliberate
☐ More responsive	or	☐ more self-controlled
☐ More improvised	or	☐ more prepared
☐ More spontaneous	or	☐ more rehearsed
☐ More intimate	or	☐ more distant
☐ More unrestrained	or	☐ more cautious
☐ More dramatic	or	☐ more proper
☐ More flexible	or	☐ more precise
☐ More feeling	or	☐ more thinking
☐ More people-oriented	or	☐ more task-oriented
☐ More impulsive	or	☐ more diplomatic
☐ More flamboyant	or	☐ more down-to-earth
☐ More warm	or	☐ more cool

Column C total _____

Scoring

1. Total the checks in **Column B**. On the horizontal line that follows, find this number and draw a vertical line through it.

2. Total the checks in **Column C**. On the vertical line, find this number and draw a horizontal line through it until the two lines intersect.

3. Circle the word in that quadrant. Read about this communication style in the following chart and see how well it describes you.

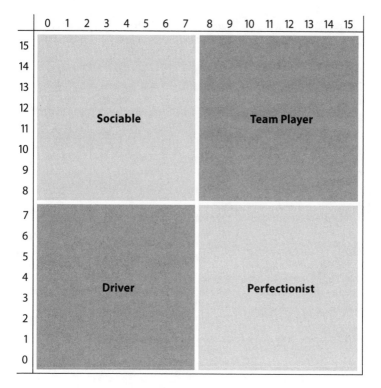

The Four Communication Styles

	Driver	Sociable	Team Player	Perfectionist
Appearance	Businesslike, fast-moving, blunt, direct	Stylish, disorganized, talkative, animated	Casual, conforming, quieter, easygoing	Precise, solemn, straitlaced
Overall behavior	Confident, impatient, changeable, pragmatic, forward	People-oriented, dramatic, creative, friendly, charismatic	Folksy, supportive, loyal, dependable, agreeable	Accurate, prudent, reserved, vigilant, persistent
Describes self as	Adventuresome, skillful, competitive	Communicative, feeling, forgiving	Responsible, helpful, dependable	Predictable, correct, fact finder
Wants to be the	Boss	Jester	Diplomat	Superior
Strengths	Decisive, efficient, leadership	Sensitive, kind, optimistic	Likable, steadfast, patient	Precise, organized, scrupulous
Convince them by telling them	What it does, when it will happen, what it will cost	How their status will rise, who else has it, how it will give them attention	How their personal relationships and security will be affected	Justify it logically, give attention to detail, back up with evidence
Needs to improve on	Intimidation, alienating others	Impatience, impracticability	Sentimentality, indecisiveness	Stubbornness, skepticism
Under stress they will	Attack, bully, dictate, dominate, push, boss	Humiliate; become sarcastic; talk longer, more, and faster	Accommodate, conform, submit, acquiesce	Withdraw, flee, retreat, get even later
Their payoff for their actions	Feels superior, others submit to their wishes	Appears influential, is the center of attention	Little or no risk to them, they have the illusion of harmony	Appears consistent, undeviating, feels prepared and superior

	Driver	Sociable	Team Player	Perfectionist
Others irritate them by being	Incompetent, indecisive, inadequate, wishy-washy	In a rut, monotonous, uninspired, boring, having no sense of humor	Unresponsive, impatient, brisk, restless, confronting	Imprecise, inaccurate, flamboyant, ambiguous
Get what you want by	Say to them, "I'll bet you can't;" support their goals	Give them applause and recognition, support their ideas, act with more energy	Displaying sincerity and trustworthiness; support their feelings	Say to them, "Do it a better way;" support their work
Best way to work with them	Give them freedom; be efficient and businesslike	Be friendly, fun, excited; give them creative jobs	Be casual, sincere, open; slow down and listen to them	Be correct, logical; tie old ideas to new ones
In an intimate relationship	Be bold, exciting, zestful, generous, physical	Be romantic, sensuous, ardent, loving, empathetic	Be predictable, loyal, secure, family-oriented	Be uncomplicated, sensible, reasonable
Theme song	"I Did It My Way"	"Celebration"	"Lean on Me"	"It's Hard to Be Humble"
Birth order	First	Last	Middle	Only
Sticking point	The need for control, power, and authority	The need for recognition and social acceptance	The need for harmony and lack of conflict or friction	The need for order, perfection, keeping the status quo
How to let it go	Back off, find a less aggressive way to get your way	Shut up sooner and longer, make an effort to listen better	Set boundaries, say *no* more often without explaining	Be slower to disagree, correct others, or be precise

Learning About Your Lion

Now that you know what your personal communication style is, it's time to learn more about your lion's. The way you get control is to create chemistry between you and your lion. Creating chemistry is knowing more about the other person than she knows about herself. The first step is to focus. Get your particular lion in your sights and focus on what they do, how you respond, and what's in it for you if things change. Do not skip this step—everything is built upon your innate knowledge of the situation.

Finish the following statements:

The person in my life that I consider difficult is

_____ .

The specific things he does or says that drive me wild are _____ .

I mostly handle the situation by _____ .

It is important that this situation change because

_____ .

If the situation changes for the better, I benefit by

_____ .

Circle ten of the following words or phrases that most *closely describe him or her.*

Disorganized	Possessive
Scatterbrained	Complacent or lenient
Talkative or animated	Patient or calming
Sarcastic	Overpromises
Phony or theatrical	Underdelivers
Stretches truth or lies	Accommodating
Practical joker	Avoids confrontation
Self-promoting	Considerate
Impulsive	No opinions
Emotional	Predictable
Has status symbols	Perfectionist
Makes blunt statements	Overanalytical
Restless	Resists change
Demanding	Nitpicker
Arrogant	Complains or whines
Outspoken	Negative or wet blanket
Quick to react	Seeks solid proof
Aggressive	Noncommunicative
Egocentric	Nags
Argumentative	Expressionless

Scoring

1. Draw a vertical line between the two columns and draw a horizontal line under the word pair Emotional/Predictable. Label the quadrants as in the scoring for your personal communication style—upper left "Sociable," upper right "Team Player," lower left "Driver," lower right "Perfectionist."

2. Note the quadrant where most of the circled words are located. This indicates your lion's communication style. If you have an equal number of circled words in more than one quadrant, your lion is a combination of these two styles. Read the descriptions of your lion's communication style to learn more.

Speaking a New Language

The secret to communicating with others, dealing with a difficult person, and taming your lion is to *speak their language, not yours.* It's as if we all have our own radio frequency. In order to be heard by another, you must be broadcasting on that person's communication frequency.

Utilize your knowledge of the four communication styles and the following guidelines. You'll find yourself hearing and being heard by the lions in your life.

Establishing Comfort Level

The beginning of any conversation can set the tone, dictate the direction, and often predict the outcome. Begin by speaking their language or broadcasting on the communication frequency on which they're listening. Your goal is to make them comfortable, not establish your foothold.

▶ **Driver.** Get to the point fast: "My reason for being here is . . ."
▶ **Sociable.** Start with small talk focusing on their prestige: "I heard that the sale closed because of your stellar efforts."
▶ **Team Player.** Make them feel comfortable with more informal talk: "How is your family doing since the move?"
▶ **Perfectionist.** Get down to business fairly fast, and put them in the role of the expert: "What do you think about the comparison study?"

Determining Needs

Demonstrating you're *interested* in the other person before you show how *interesting* you are is not only common courtesy but also good business sense. Before you tell them what *you* want, determine what *they* need.

▶ **Driver.** Be serious, and include some probes that get them talking about results and efficiency: "What can I do to make this chore easier for you?"
▶ **Sociable.** Keep them excited by *being* excited, and your enthusiasm will spark theirs. How you say it is as important as what you say: "This is an amazing project, isn't it!"
▶ **Team Player.** Exhibit your sincerity by including some questions that focus on team spirit or morale: "What do you think the group needs to really improve the situation?"
▶ **Perfectionist.** Stay on task with minimum small talk. Include some questions that allow them to share knowledge and expertise: "What do you think are the top three priorities in this situation?"

Suggesting Benefits That Meet Needs

Benefit statements are the answer to someone's asking you, "What's in it for me?" or "Tell me why I should do this." They meet needs of the other person, not you.

▶ **Driver.** Use some benefit statements that emphasize efficiency, profits, cost savings: "This system will save you $85,000 the first quarter, improving your bottom line 23 percent."
▶ **Sociable.** Use some benefit statements that show how they will look good or save effort: "With our service, there will be less hassle and downtime for you."
▶ **Team Player.** Use some benefit statements that emphasize team harmony and morale: "Our service will help your team be more efficient without sacrificing the spirit you've carefully built."
▶ **Perfectionist.** Use some benefit statements that stress logic and security: "The three-part encryption, automatic backup, and off-site storage features of this program ensure that your data's safety will be protected."

Meeting Resistance or Objections

Resistance and objections are just other people telling you that you haven't made the benefits *to them* clear. If you experience "roadblock" behavior from any of these four communication styles, here are suggestions for dealing with them.

▶ **Driver.** Don't take their bluntness personally. Be as direct as they are, but don't get into an argument. Appeal to logic by using evidence: "You have a point, and let me show you some studies."

▶ **Sociable.** Accept their feelings or doubts and use a lot of feeling statements: "It's only natural you'd feel that way, but I feel . . ."

▶ **Team Player.** Accept and share their feelings, and promise friendship and helpfulness: "I would feel the same way in your position, and I promise I will . . ."

▶ **Perfectionist.** Accept and share their logic, and give additional data to reassure them: "I understand that you need 1, 2, and 3 to implement this. Here are recent journal articles to substantiate my process."

Getting a Commitment

Occasionally in your career it will be crucial for your lion or lions to buy into a project or sale you are spearheading. You need assurance from them that their answer is yes and they are behind you. The following strategies might give you a better shot.

▶ **Driver.** Quickly and briefly review options, and let them make the decision: "I believe your options are . . ."

▶ **Sociable.** Use your excitement to inspire them to action: "Wow! Just think of how . . ." Then, ask directly for what you want while they are enthusiastic.

▶ **Team Player.** Detail how they can take action, support their decision in a sincere way, and get a definite commitment for action, since they may otherwise postpone a decision: "I feel that we agree on these four points, and I have the form here for you to approve."

▶ **Perfectionist.** Offer options and help them prioritize to make a decision, and support their decision with logic: "The facts speak for themselves."

Following Up on Details

How you follow up with the details will set the stage for the ease or difficulty of your next encounter with your lion. Savvy salespeople know that selling to an existing client is much easier than finding a new one, and advertisers report that it is *five times* more expensive to attract a new customer than to keep an existing one.

▶ **Driver.** They will appreciate the efficiency and attention.

▶ **Sociable.** They will appreciate how your follow-up work saves them trouble and effort and makes them look good to others.

▶ **Team Player.** They will appreciate the personal attention that your diligent follow-up work indicates.

▶ **Perfectionist.** They will appreciate your consistent follow-up work and reliability.

Personality Types to Be Tamed

In his book *Don't Tick Off the Gators*, my friend Jim Grigsby relates stories and lessons of men and women triumphing over problems that are menacing, slippery, and frightening—like gators lurking in the swamp. He believes that dealing with difficult people under ideal circumstances (or in a corporate environment) requires that you have a plan, a feasibility analysis, and an 80 percent probability of success before implementing your plan. Even in a crisis, a sixty-forty success ratio may be enough to go forward.

These basic skills are similar to those of martial arts/ physical self-defense.

▶ **Keep a low center of gravity.** Keep yourself centered and balanced as much as possible.

▶ **Take care of yourself first.** Think of an aviation emergency: you must put on your own oxygen mask before attempting to help others.

▶ **Be light on your feet.** Pick the right place and time to defend yourself.

▶ **Protect life and limb.** Don't try to be a dead hero—remove yourself when necessary and just get out of there.

▶ **Brute strength doesn't prevail.** Use your opponents' energy and make it work for you.

Here are tips for dealing with the most common lions you encounter in the most productive, least time-sucking way possible.

Bullies

Bullies demand, intimidate, overrun, or railroad you into decisions you regret later. These decisions often lead to you doing more work and increasing your busyness. If you let them intimidate you into doing extra work, the time it takes to figure out how to please them can distract you indefinitely. They have often earned nicknames such as Sherm (as in Sherman tank), General (as in military might), or Ram (like the truck). They judge your worth on whether or not you stand up to them—literally and figuratively. Beware, though; things may get worse before they get better.

It's difficult to stand up to them right at the moment they are bullying you. Study, practice, and use this formula for heading them off at the pass. Call it your "I statement."

I feel _____ (impact on you—anger, frustration, betrayal) when you _____ (describe their behavior neutrally without emotion or judgment).

I would prefer if you would _____ (describe the preferred behavior).

If you do, _____ (the payoff for them).

You may not be aware that _____ (collateral damage this behavior causes).

Thanks, I'm glad we had this talk.

Here is an example:

I feel frustrated when you stand at my desk, raise your voice, throw your pen, and shake your finger at me. I would prefer that you talk to me in private before the time pressures shorten our fuses. If you do, you'll actually get what you want sooner and with higher quality. You may not be aware, but when this happens, I am so affected that I lose the whole afternoon.

Note: Be careful to *not* use the phrasing "If you don't, _____" because negative consequences sound very much like threats.

Exploders, Tantrum Throwers, Yellers, and Loudmouths

When someone explodes, your natural instinct is to push back. Don't! Emotions are usually so high that solutions won't come until you let the person wind down. This is a battle that even if you win, you lose. Instead, here is what to do:

▶ Adopt a neutral stance—face them with both feet on the ground and give them nothing to fuel their fire. Picture them as an inflated balloon that you let go . . . *fsssuuu* all around the room. Let them wind down—don't interrupt or touch them.

▶ Rise slowly if you're seated.

▶ Maintain eye contact—let your eye contact wander around their upper face, don't stare like a zombie.

▶ Slow your breathing—your fight-or-flight system increases your heart and breathing rates.

▶ Cross your arms or hold your hand out with the "stop sign" gesture if you're feeling strong.

▶ Snap them out of it with the sweetest word they know—their own name. "Sylvia!" "Ivan!" The worst thing you can say is "Calm down," "Wait a minute," or "Stop." Instead, try one of the following:

   ▶ Ask for a solution: "I can see that this is a really big problem to you—what can we do together to help solve it?" or "What would you like me to do to help solve it?"

   ▶ Ask, "Is there anything else?" Don't let them play on your instinct to defend.

   ▶ Ask them to leave: "I feel overwhelmed right now. I would like you to come back when you're less angry."

   ▶ Leave yourself: "I'm going to leave now and I'll come back when we can talk about it in a little bit more productive manner." Behave with silent strength.

After someone's blown up, make an appointment or go in and see them as soon as they're calm again. Tell it like it is using your "I statement": "I feel very frustrated when you stand in my department yelling and get my whole group upset. I would prefer that you not do this in the future."

Know-It-Alls

You find them everywhere—the person who has already made up his mind about the situation and he's going to let you know it in no uncertain terms. Perhaps you work with someone who thinks she already knows the solution, and there doesn't seem any way to open her mind to an alternative. Whether they really do know it all or they just think they do, stick with this formula.

- ▶ Be totally present. Make verbal attends (noises) such as "ah huh," "OK," "right," "sure," and "hmm."
- ▶ Lean forward and nod slowly.
- ▶ Paraphrase or repeat what they've said—even if you don't believe it.
- ▶ "Columbo" them: "Ah, could you, wait, wait just a minute, I'm not quite sure when you said . . ." Watch Peter Falk in the classic reruns of "Columbo." He was a master of allowing people to speak until they hung themselves. He didn't go head-to-head with the know-it-all, he just let them talk, often acting a bit dense or slow-witted.
- ▶ Thank and acknowledge them: "Thanks, that's an excellent point."
- ▶ Point out working together. "Gee, your idea sounds great. Let's work together and see how we might be able to combine what I've just mentioned and what you brought up."

Alicia was negotiating a land sale contract for her buyers with the sellers' attorney. He was nearly a caricature of a "bad" attorney—portly, bald, loud, chauvinistic, and overbearing. She felt her blood pressure rising, yet she stayed calm and repeatedly said, "That hasn't been my experience" to every idea he offered.

The attorney probably got so fed up and frustrated with her just making this one comment that he finally blew up and said, "Well, what the hell is your experience?" She very calmly took her papers, stood up, and proceeded to counter with, "In the twenty-three transactions like this that I've closed since January, I've found that all parties settle upon this formula."

Complainers and Whiners

A well-handled complaint creates loyalty and repeat business. According to a survey from the U.S. Office of Consumer Affairs, most—more than 70 percent—of consumers with service problems *do not* complain. But when they *did* and their gripes were resolved, 70 percent said they would reuse that product. When complaints were *not* resolved, fewer than half said they would purchase the product or service again. When the loss was greater than two hundred dollars, 91 percent of those who did not complain *just stopped using it.*

Complainers can take up time reiterating their complaints, requiring you to solve their problems and shaking confidence. This all adds to your busyness and stress. You can tame your complainer lion with these simple steps.

Listen for Clues. Make a commitment to listen to the complainer fully before you interrupt, solve, or correct the problem. Often we interrupt or ignore complainers, making them worse. After all, you're busy and you need to move on. Asking for more complaints is not a sick desire for more pain but a way to smoke out the real complaint. Ever noticed how some people whine around a problem? Think of them as a full balloon needing to be relieved of the hot air.

Repeat the Complaint. Once Mr. or Ms. Verypicky has dumped on you, take all the information and condense it into a few short sentences. You will be paraphrasing them, *not* parroting. Begin this paraphrasing by saying, "What I hear you saying is . . ." or "It's my understanding that your main concern is . . ." and then summarize the points as you understand them.

Put It in Their Lap. This is the key to converting them. Before you start with your solution, ask them to solve the problem. This is like a tennis game when your opponent smashes a serve to you. What do you do? Return it! Before you say, "This is nuts," consider their viewpoint. The whole time they've been grumbling to themselves and others, they've already started "shoulding" on you. Whether they've told you or not, they're thinking, "She should do this" or "What should have been done is that." All you're doing is giving them permission—and that builds relationship. The faster a positive relationship is established, the closer you are to converting them to your ally.

Limit Your Response. The ball's now in their court, and they blast it back with the most ridiculous (undoable, expensive, illegal) solution. Do not show emotion, outrage, or smugness. Rather, paraphrase their solution and tell them what you're going to do. "I understand you'd like the manager shot, your money refunded, a new product at no charge, and the company closed. What I am prepared to do is . . ." Limit your response to what you *will* do.

Loop Back When Possible. If you see them later, don't avoid their gaze, hide, or turn the other way. Instead, smile, approach them, and say, "I really appreciate you bringing that to my attention." Add where appropriate, "I hope it was resolved to your satisfaction." This is what martial arts students refer to as "honoring your opponent." It's a golden opportunity to solidify the relationship, making you "dependable" and going a long way to making them your ally in future situations.

The greatest bonus to converting the complainer will be the formation of a bond between you and that person. Yes, you'll actually become closer to that person—and that's a good thing. The *Harvard Business Review* reported that service is your only strategic weapon for differentiating yourself. In these days when you must do more with less, isn't it good to know that converting a complainer is a skill that will dramatically distinguish you as a professional and valuable member of the team?

Drama Queens (and Kings)

Having worked in advanced life support, I *know* what real drama is. Present me with an unconscious person, and I can check vitals, initiate CPR, and start an IV simultaneously. When someone falls off (or is unloaded from) a horse in our barn, I'm flying across the arena barking orders, grabbing the loose horse, and doing first aid on the person about the time most people are thinking, "Ah, did something just happen?"

Present me with people who have some commotion or atrocity going on, and I have an opinion how they can solve it. I'll try to gently suggest what to do. If that doesn't work, I'll try another solution. After they do nothing I suggest and I'm worn out from trying, I finally get it! *They don't want my help; they just want their drama!*

To a drama queen or king (DQ or DK), everything is cause for high alert. They can stir up anxiety in even the most centered person and halt production in the smoothest-running department. A DQ or DK might look and act calmly themselves, but they've always got *something* dramatic, tumultuous, or just plain weird going on. At first, you try to be their friend, because you are enlightened, kind, and compassionate. You listen, you empathize, and you try to help. Soon you find yourself irritated by their very presence. You tell yourself, "Be kinder, they're going through a rough patch." But, then the patch turns into a long period of time. Soon, when you see them dancing in your peripheral vision, you want to say "What now?!" You've even thought of smacking them with tough love. Rather than facing possible assault charges, though, there is a better way.

The drama queen has identified you as someone she can engage in the drama that is happening to her. Best-case scenario is to *not* get engaged in the first place but, instead, to subtly give her the impression that you're unavailable for *whatever it is*. Often, all it takes is a "Hello, how are you?" to suck you in. When you find yourself caught in the drama net, you can keep yourself untangled if you

▶ Look at them directly.
▶ Make no comment or verbal noise.
▶ Offer no suggestion to help.

If you *must* say something, try

▶ "Hmmmm" (nodding slowly), *or*
▶ "I, ah, just don't know" (shaking your head slowly and sympathetically), *and*
▶ "Gosh, it beats me, I need to get this finished" (turn back to your work).

Outside of an office setting, stonewalling a drama queen could lead to some kind of blowup. After all, you are denying them what they crave most: attention. But the fact of simply being in a professional setting is enough to ensure that your unwillingness to get sucked into drama will not lead to higher-level drama. Like everyone else, drama kings and queens do want to stay employed.

Unreliables

There are those folks in your work life you can't count on. They promise but don't deliver. Even when they say, "Sure, I'll have the report in the morning," or "I'll pick that up when I go to the field office," you know it's probably not going to happen. Here's how to keep them on the up-and-up:

▶ Be realistic. "I know this kind of commitment is hard for most people. Are you sure you can make it?"
▶ Find the middle ground. "I know we agreed on two weeks, but I'd be OK with three weeks if that would help you."
▶ Get them to recap the agreement by asking them to explain their understanding of the important facts.
▶ Tie their commitment to their sense of personal honor. "Do I have your word on that?" "I know I can count on you for that."
▶ If necessary, put it in writing, and both parties sign.

Critics

These are the people who make snide comments or criticisms. When they're called on it, they reply innocently, "Oh, I was just *kidding*, can't you take a joke?" Or, they are the champions of the dramatic sign, eye roll, or thumbs-down. Their attacks are just as damaging as those of the "exploders." Sometimes even more damaging, because the attack is more like a laser—pointed and concentrated on you directly. Try some of these methods to deflect the shot.

▶ Questions give them an alternative to sniping. "Do you have something to add?"

▶ Smoke them out. "That sounded like an insult, did you mean it that way?"

▶ Negative inquiry. "The 'stupidest idea' . . . What exactly causes you to say that?"

▶ Expose the covert gesture. "What did you mean by giving that 'so-so' gesture?"

▶ In a group, seek consensus of the criticism. "Does anyone else see it that way?"

▶ When the group agrees, ask, "OK, can you be more specific?"

▶ Ask for more criticism. "Anything else?"

Listen to what they say. If it's valid criticism and not just a cheap shot, the sharpshooter may have come up with something concrete you can work on. If they're just taking potshots at you, it may exhaust their behavior. If they're constantly being called on it to explain themselves, they may have a tendency to stop these attacks on you, in public anyway.

Sometimes it's a friend who lobs these zingers at you, as a way to validate that you two are close. Address "friendly fire" in private, by saying, "Remember, when you said _____? What I really need from you is your support, not your criticism."

Saboteurs and Thunder-Stealers

Don't you hate those people who take credit for your ideas? There are some points to remember if you're in a highly competitive situation or have saboteurs in your midst.

▶ **Don't** present a great idea casually passing in the hall or as a tag-on to someone's similar idea. **Do** formally present your ideas to the right people with forethought and planning.

▶ **Don't** downplay your ideas or work! If you have a great idea, **do** put it succinctly in writing (one page) and make an appointment to present it to the right person: "I need ten minutes to discuss a new idea I have for streamlining the system." Let him or her know that *you* think it's a great idea.

▶ **Don't** wait until a project is over to let everybody know what your contribution was. **Do** let all of your colleagues know your part and that you expect credit for what you've done.

▶ **Don't** forget to create buzz for your ideas. **Do** make sure that the grapevine is aware of your activities. Every department has a grapevine—learn it and use it.

▶ **Don't** hide your involvement in a project. **Do** work on your own personal publicity campaign—put good or important news in writing and let people know what you're doing, being as visible as possible within the group.

▶ **Don't** let yourself fade into the background. **Do** speak for your department. If you have problems speaking in front of groups, join Toastmasters (toastmasters.org).

▶ **Don't** skimp on compliments, appreciation, and recognition. **Do** give credit to others when they're doing a good job. Send handwritten thank-you notes if they deserve it.

▶ **Don't** forget the power of proof and the written word. **Do** document yourself and back up like crazy.

"No People" and Negative Analysts

You need to distinguish between genuine "no people" and "negative analysts"—one hurts, and the other helps. Negative analysts are contingency planners—they say, "Here's the problem, this is the rub, and this is what we should do about it." They are self-appointed troubleshooters bringing solutions, not just griping and criticism. Genuine "no people," on the other hand, bring problems, complaints, criticism, and gripes *without* solutions or ideas. Here is how you deal with them:

- Acknowledge what they say and counter it with a positive statement. "You could be right, and this is the smartest group we've ever dealt with."
- Don't get sucked into their negativity. Instead, say something like, "That hasn't been my experience."
- Don't argue. Chances are they've always been a negative person, and you're not going to change their mind by arguing.
- Ask them for solutions. "What do you think would work here?"
- Examine the negativity closely. "What's the worst that can happen?"
- Reprogram them if you have the energy and love. Meet with them in private and say, "I've noticed you've hit a rough patch, and you might not be aware of how negative you've become. I don't think that this is who you really are." Frequently, when they are made aware of how they've slipped into being a "no person," they take it upon themselves to improve.

Indecisives and Stallers

First cousins to a "no person," indecisives and stallers avoid making decisions. They drive you crazy by wasting so much time researching something to death, looking at all the options, and wanting a perfect result. These folks can stall a sale and limit your productivity if you let them.

If you want an answer or decision from those over-aiming lions:

▶ Give them no more than two or three alternatives
  and your opinion as to which one is best and why you
  think so. "We can go with one of these three logos.
  I think the middle one most suits all our needs for
  clarity, color, and professionalism."
▶ Give them a deadline and the decision or action you will
  take if they pass that time limit. "If I don't hear from you
  by tomorrow afternoon, I will proceed with my choice."
▶ Make a pro and con list with them. "In situations like
  this, I like to look at both sides to this decision. You've
  mentioned 1, 2, and 3 as reasons for going ahead (write
  under pro). What else might we consider?"
▶ Make a decision with their help. "It seems like there are
  more reasons to go forward. I'll draw up the paperwork
  this afternoon and return for your approval."

Unresponsives

Silence is powerful. When silent, unresponsive or passive
people use it to manipulate you, wiggle out of a hot seat, or
blow you off—you need to be clever and persistent. The Silent
Clam is staring at you; your major task is to get him to talk.

▶ Set an appropriate time limit for how long you're going
  to wait until dealing with them.
▶ Ask for their opinion, "What do you think is the best
  way to proceed?"
▶ Give them your friendly silent stare—you're looking at
  them expectantly, with a pleasant expression, raising
  your eyebrows, nodding your head, smiling slightly, or
  waving them on with your hand. "OK, go on."

▶ You can figuratively step to the side. "I'm expecting you to comment, and you're not. What does that indicate?"

▶ You can counter their "I don't know" with "What else?" to engage them further.

▶ As your last resort, check your interpretation of their silent response. "You look angry (frustrated, annoyed, etc.), am I right?"

▶ If the unresponsive person would rather leave than talk with you, you can very casually and firmly say or do the following:

  ▶ "No, not now, I still have a few things on my mind."

  ▶ Wait them out until the time limit you set earlier. "I have twenty minutes to discuss this with you, so I'll wait while you gather your thoughts."

  ▶ Pay attention to out-the-door comments. Therapists know the last ten minutes of a therapeutic hour is when all the good stuff comes out.

  ▶ Reschedule the conversation, "It seems like we can't go anywhere with this right now. Let's pick up tomorrow between 10 and 11. Let me know if this is *not* a good time."

  ▶ After several attempts, tell them what you're going to do. "I am going to write a report as to what I believe is happening and what can be done. If you don't respond, I'll assume you agree, and we will meet in one month to check on progress."

Post-Battle Analysis

My horse-training mentor has a favorite saying: "Get your go and get your whoa." When you get control of the horse's "go" and "stop," you'll be in charge and stay out of danger. Even after millions of years of evolution, being a prey animal, the horse runs first and asks questions later. Due to its size and power, a horse's "stop" needs to be absolute and unquestioned.

My American Quarter Horse mare, Maggie, is so young and fit that all I have to do is gently squeeze her with my calves like a toothpaste tube for her to go. The "stop" needed work. If she is "spooked," she can go from zero to forty in a split second. I like speed as much as the next cowgirl, but this may be leading us right *into* danger. Once she's bolting, forget about yelling "whoa," sitting deep in the saddle, or pulling on the reins—I need an emergency hand brake! The only way to stop a four-legged, half-ton crackhead from killing both of us is to disengage the motor.

The power in a horse is the hind end, and quarter horses have the biggest butts of all the breeds. My skinny little arms are no match for all that muscle—but my brain is. I was taught to grab one rein as close to her mouth as possible and pull steadily toward where the side seam of my jeans meets the waistband. She responds by disengaging her back end (the motor), turning, and slowing to a stop.

When I was learning this maneuver, I put duct tape at the ultimate spot on each rein so that I could program my brain. I practiced *hundreds* of times in many different situations until it was an ingrained response. Now, in that split second between her panicked intake of breath and the missile launch, I automatically reach and pull.

My friend Jim Grigsby reminds me of a crucial step *after* you deal with a difficult person, the post-battle analysis. Jim suggests asking yourself these key questions.

- ▶ Did I cause the problem? (by not knowing enough about the other person)
- ▶ Did I create the environment that allowed it to flourish? (by ignoring the problem, hoping it would go away)
- ▶ What was the cause of the crisis? (a lack of communication, bad information)

▶ How did I respond to each event or stage? (learning when to hold 'em and when to fold 'em)
▶ Can this situation be prevented in the future? (learn a new skill and practice before the crisis)
▶ What can I learn from this experience? (you are able to take care of yourself and stay out of danger)

When dealing with a difficult person, analyze the problem, the causes, and your reactions. This is your way to *take responsibility* for getting yourself into the mess in the first place. As with a runaway horse, you can prevail over someone bigger, stronger, and more formidable with knowledge, courage, and practice.

Chapter 8

The Care and Feeding of Coworkers and Bosses

The greatest good you can do for another is not to share your riches but to reveal to him his own.

—Benjamin Disraeli

In the previous chapter, we addressed the personality types that you'll come across at work. Let's take a closer look at your direct supervisor and immediate coworkers. If you want to help return civility to the workplace, you need to pay special attention to the people closest to you.

You may not admire, respect, or even like your coworkers and bosses, but often the best teams are made of people with disparate talents and skills. Each person brings his or her unique personality that accompanies their job competence. The likelihood of friction—or downright conflict—is great. Whether you're at the top of the ladder or the bottom, honing your relationship skills saves you time and busyness.

This summary below is a quick overview of the quality of relationships you can expect with different combinations of communication styles. It's important to have a highly developed sense of yourself so that you can use your powers of observation to make your working relationships with others more straightforward, satisfying, and productive.

Styles	Great	Good	Fair	Poor
Driver/Driver			X	
Driver/Sociable			X	
Driver/Team Player	X			
Driver/Perfectionist			X	
Sociable/Sociable				X
Sociable/Team Player	X			
Sociable/Perfectionist		X		
Team Player/Team Player	X			
Team Player/Perfectionist	X			
Perfectionist/Perfectionist	X			

What Is Your Coworker's Communication Style?

Most of the time you can do your work and proceed at your natural pace and style. When your busy dial is turned to "high" and you're getting stressed, your radar will alert you to your particular lions. This is the time that you need to broadcast *on their frequency* so you'll be heard and understood—heading off conflict or alienation. Use this table to learn more about your coworkers in order to save time and busyness and return heart and soul to your workplace.

If you're voluntarily about to enter a working relationship with someone, wouldn't you be interested in compatibility between your style and hers? Isn't it better to match a job with a person than to have that person struggle with a position that he doesn't fit (or doesn't like)? What have you learned about your coworkers who are stressing you by making more *busy* for you? More important, what are you going to do about it?

Communication Style Characteristics

	Driver	Sociable	Team Player	Perfectionist
Strengths at work	Doer, thorough, hard-charging, effective, assertive, pragmatic, achiever, über-busy, knowledgeable, objective	Passionate, animated, charismatic, creative, enthusiastic, eager, raring to go, busy without direction, keen, often hyperactive	Supportive, steady, empathetic, kind, dependable, sincere, loyal, not rushed, pensive, comfortable, nurturing	Organized, systematic, industrious, meticulous, scheduled, prudent, persistent, predictable
Weaknesses at work	Uncompromising, pressuring, bossy, domineering, harsh, self-involved, shortsighted, impatient	Impatient, egotistical, opinionated, loud, impractical, talkative, unstructured, naive, disorganized	Sentimental, submits under pressure, subjective, avoids conflict, aimless, hesitant, timid	Impersonal, fussy, withdraws under pressure, indecisive, skeptical, loner, predictable
Outlook on time	Deliberate, conscious, start and end early	What's time? little time consciousness, usually late	Flexible, unconcerned with time	Precise, start and end on time, digitally correct
Dress code	Dark, conservative, solids, powerful	Trendy, flashy, labels, jewelry	Comfortable, warm colors, favorites	Sensible, grays, unfashionable
Work energy	Multitasking, restless, serious, unemotional	Enthusiastic, excitable, impulsive, wide energy swings	Concerned, friendly, receptive, open, loving, warm	Low-key, quiet, reserved, stoic, undemonstrative
Workspace	Impressive, gadgets, awards, large furniture	Generally messy, odd furniture, closets and drawers bulging	Comfortable, casual, homey, welcoming	Clean, organized, lined up and perpendicular

	Driver	Sociable	Team Player	Perfectionist
Speech pattern	Fast, loud, direct, abrupt, bottom line	Rapid, joking, stories, inflective, gestures	Warm, folksy, easy, personal, asking	Careful, measured, quiet, accurate
Usual complaint	I don't have enough time; this is what we should do.	People don't listen to me or follow my directions.	Can't we all just get along? Stop arguing and fighting.	Someone is not following the rules and plan.
Thoughts on change	Already has enough to do, but OK if it gets immediate results.	Why not, can't fight it, and besides, change makes the world go 'round.	Can change if it goes smoothly and everyone else agrees.	Stop! How can it be done right if things keep changing?
Evaluation of self	I get more done than anyone.	I keep this workplace fun and positive.	I fit in, and people really like me.	I keep this place organized and correct.

Relationship Combinations

One of the best assistants I've ever had nearly didn't make it through the first month with me. Her tasks were not time-sensitive, so she usually arrived long after I'd dug into my projects for the day. Walking into the door, she usually had some (admittedly hilarious) story about caring for her elderly aunt or managing a beachside apartment complex. I dropped a few not-so-subtle hints about having a lot of work to do and not having time to chat, but I couldn't tell whether she picked up on them or not.

It wasn't until I looked at the combination of our personality styles and how it affected working together that I appreciated the gem that she was. She was highly sociable, and in the office, I was in my Driver mode. I needed the softening and lightening up that she brought to my business, plus she was exceptionally organized, could type ninety words a minute, answer the phone, and work better than anyone I'd met. I took her morning arrival as a needed break, so we spent some time together, and I came to look forward to her stories. She ended up staying with me for seven highly functional (and successful) years.

There are many relationship combinations between you and your coworkers that might stir up your *busy*, drain you dry, keep you from doing your best, or make you less productive. You can also learn to polish up and appreciate your high-value combinations (HVCs). You may think that your HVCs are annoying, create more "busy," and waste your time, but you can make them constructive, ultimately improving your productivity.

Most of us are not aware of how deep-seated our personality is. When talking about difficult relationships, nearly all my seminar students believe that *their* relationship style is not the one causing their "busy"—it's the *other* person. This is partially true. It's the *combination* of them that affects the way you work. Take a look at how the combinations play out.

For Drivers

If you are a Driver, here's how you work with . . .

▶ **Drivers.** There may be an undercurrent of competition between you, but you appreciate, admire, and respect them because they seem as smart as you. Your juices get flowing around them because they like *busy* as much as you. Trying to top, compete with, or overpower them will only frustrate you and waste your time. Compliment their ideas and work on lowering your aggressive and competitive tendencies.

▶ **Sociables.** You might find them helpful and worthwhile, but their tendency to be chatty can get on your nerves, distract you, and waste your time. Ask direct questions and develop your exit strategies: "Thanks, I need to be somewhere."

▶ **Team Players.** You often get irritated at their laid-back attitude, but this can be an HVC since they are dependable, solid workers. They appear to waste your time by looking at all sides of the project and making sure they're doing it like you want. Working together will be a positive experience if you tell them what you want, give them appreciation, and sincerely recognize the value of their loyalty.

▶ **Perfectionists.** In your mind they are picky, lack the big picture, and waste your time with questions, details, complaints, conflicts, and minutiae. Slow down, assure them of the details, and don't try to be their good friend or mentor.

For Sociables

If you are a Sociable, here's how you work with . . .

▶ **Drivers.** They might seem formal, pompous, and too businesslike, restlessly stomping your good cheer with their need to stay on schedule and get things done. Stay out of their way and don't try to lighten them up or make them your good friend; they just want to see productivity.

▶ **Sociables.** You two can talk and laugh the day away, getting *nothing* done. You each want to be queen of the castle, so careful with the competition. Set time limits on your interactions and be vigilant about staying off the topic of gossip.

▶ **Team Players.** You might find yourself irritated at their wishy-washiness or their consistent, even moods, but this can be an HVC. They will keep you grounded and more productive by their constancy and model how to be kind and considerate.

▶ **Perfectionists.** You might find them boring and uncreative and consider them a nitpicker, nag, or stick-in-the-mud. They seem to waste your time by bugging you for details, facts, and accuracy. Be a little less playful and talkative with them and stop trying to make them light, playful, or less serious.

For Team Players

If you are a Team Player, here's how you work with . . .

▶ **Drivers.** You might think this person has perfected BSing to an art form. However, this working relationship can be an HVC. They will stand up for you when you're both on the same page and be your protector. If you need help from them, be prepared to prove your value. Ignore any of their bluntness and don't take it personally.

▶ **Sociables.** This person will challenge your time lines and schedule, but they are a positive force with their energy and optimism. Get their commitments in writing, set false deadlines with wiggle room, and use their wild and unique creativity.

▶ **Team Players.** You are suspicious of their loyalty to others in a position of authority and their don't-make-waves policy. Working closely with them can be an HVC because they are from the same "Planet Good" as you—being fair, flexible, and agreeable. Show interest in their personal life and goals and be specific about what you want and need from them.

▶ **Perfectionists.** You might feel that these people take pleasure in making you as busy as possible, but this can be an HVC. Their need for details, documentation, and lack of emotion makes work so much *work*. Give up trying to make them more cheerful, and use them to focus on the task. When you do exactly what you said you would and answer questions as specifically as possible, they'll make you look like a star.

For Perfectionists

If you are a Perfectionist, here's how you work with . . .

▶ **Drivers.** These people drive you wild (pun intended) with their laissez-faire attitude toward details and their need for speed. They make more work for you because you believe that lack of attention to the fine print will be the downfall of the company. Move quickly through your points, be prepared to prove the value of your logic, and attempt to be flexible with resolutions.

▶ **Sociables.** You might consider this talkative social butterfly a loose cannon. Sometimes you might even just want them to quiet down and go away. They are sensitive to the emotion behind your words, so be careful that you don't speak in a condescending or dismissive manner. When they ask, limit the amount of details you give them and be prepared for conclusions or decisions that you may never have even thought of.

▶ **Team Players.** This relationship can be an HVC if you take the lead. Searching for a consensus and wanting authorities' support, these people often submit to the most forceful person, regardless of who's correct. When you prove your point by showing that the authorities are on board, they will be your greatest champion.

▶ **Perfectionists.** This can be an HVC because you see the world identically and think (not feel) that you've found a kindred spirit. But you two can lose *whole days* getting lost in all that information and all those details. Set a timetable, have benchmarks for completion of each section or project; *someone* needs to draw some conclusions.

Gentle Persuasion of Your Boss

Many of you might have flipped right to this section because you're sure that your boss is making more "busy" for you than necessary, and it's stressing you. Here's the 411 on working with different kinds of bosses. Along with some basic info about their personality style, you'll get further faster in the organization if you know what makes them tick and what ticks them off.

When You're the Boss

Whether you've risen to management level from competence or because no one else would take the position, this is your chance to make work *work*. The more you know about yourself and others, the better and more civil the workplace will be. But, wait! Just when you have a handle on taming lions, it turns out there are a few other skills that will save you time and energy.

What Your Boss's Type Means for You

	Driver	Sociable	Team Player	Perfectionist
Meetings with them	Infrequent, impromptu, for crisis management, dictatorial	Frequent, spontaneous, ad hoc, brief; agenda not followed	Regular, scheduled, long but casual, agenda of whatever others want	Frequent, long, boring, strict agenda, focused, details and trivia
Makes decisions by	Fire first, ask questions later; alone	Fire, ready, aim	Ready, aim, fire with consensus	Aim, aim, aim until correct
Teamwork attitude	Forget about the teamwork, just get your own work done.	Teamwork is a chance to get everyone involved.	We are family! This is great.	When the team is under control, on track, and on schedule, it's great.
Fixes problems by	Kicking butt and working hard	Trying another tactic or new idea	Getting together and talking things over	New or better rules, procedures, systems
Coaching style	Watch me do it, then you go do it.	Let's try this, or that, or whatever.	We can work this out together.	Takes much time and covers details
Impress them by	Taking initiative, doing things before you're asked, respecting their authority	Being excited, conveying big picture, seeking their consent and agreement	Showing interest in personal objectives, doing your homework, getting consensus	Doing exactly what you said you would do and doing it on schedule
They promote you for	Being accessible, getting the job done	Wholeheartedly following directions	Getting along, harmony, usefulness	Following policies and procedures
They praise you for	Handling a crisis	Productivity, hard work	Exclusive information	Being steady, unflappable

▶ **Model good behavior.** Learn how to act, not *react*, to your employees' behaviors. If one calls you a horse's a**—OK, let it go. If two people do—look in the mirror. If three call you a horse's a**—buy yourself a saddle.

▶ **Listen for predators.** Learn to listen with all your senses. Ask questions and opinions, and wait for the answers. Paraphrase answers back to the speaker. Confirm what you heard.

▶ **Get commitments.** Turn a promise into a commitment by nailing it down to a specific date and time—avoid vague and unclear statements such as "as soon as possible" or "the first of the month." Follow up in writing.

▶ **Deliver hard news.** There is no magic way to make bad news less bad. Be sincere, straightforward, and sympathetic: "I need to tell you something disturbing."

▶ **Intervene.** If two people are involved in a disagreement and are incapable of reaching a solution, these elements need to be present for you to intervene:
  ▶ The desire of both parties to resolve the conflict
  ▶ The respect of both parties
  ▶ The agreement of both parties to implement resolutions

Attitude Determines Altitude

What you think of coworkers and boss helps to determine your attitude at work. Your attitude, in turn, helps to determine your productivity, your enjoyment of your job, and your stress level. Take some time to examine your relationships with your coworkers and boss(es). If you *are* the boss, strive to understand your employees before you decide on a course of action during times of ultra-busyness and high stress. Your understanding of relationships and communication skills will determine the culture of your workplace.

Work is not just some place you do a minimal job, sit around texting your friends, play "How Old Is Your Brain?" games online, have a meal, and go home. It's where you discover *you*. The late Dr. David Viscott, a popular psychiatrist, often said, "The purpose of life is to discover your gift, and the meaning of life is using it." Work is where you can discover your unique, special gift. You have a choice where you are.

One of the most charming books I've read is *Water for Elephants* by Sara Gruen. Set during the Depression on trains with a traveling circus, the story is told through flashbacks in the voice of a man in a nursing home. The elephants are the main attraction, and smart ways have to be devised to contain them. (Nothing riles up the townsfolk faster than the elephants trampling their clotheslines and decimating their gardens.)

When the elephants are small, they are restrained with a large chain around their back leg. This chain is attached to a very large post pounded into the ground or sunk into cement. The baby elephant pulls on the chain, but he is not yet strong enough to pull the post out of the ground. And as he gets older, the chain is kept the same, but he stops pulling on it because, in his mind, he is still a small elephant with a very large chain and post. He doesn't do anything about it because he thinks he has no choice.

You are not an elephant. No matter what your earlier experiences have been, you *do* have a choice. You can choose to make your workplace more civil or, better yet, a great place to work. Your attitude toward others will determine your altitude—how high or happy you'll be there—and to what prominence you'll rise. Soar, my friend!

Chapter 9

Finding Your Balance at Work

We must become the change
we want to see.

—Mahatma Gandhi

The corporate landscape is changing constantly. Keeping up with what's in, what's out, and what's expected of you is enough to unhinge even the most self-assured person. How can you expect to stay balanced at work when change and, therefore, imbalance is the norm? You cannot be first-rate at your job if eating, sleeping, and work is all you do in your life. Even though you may spend the bulk of your waking life at your job, it is not your life. Your life is *yours*. Your employer may seem to think that he owns you, but you know better. If you're chafing at the thought that you feel trapped in the chaotic busyness of your job, the time has come to take some control back and find your balance!

Prioritize and Plan to Manage Your Time

Stephen Covey's phenomenally successful book *The 7 Habits of Highly Effective People* stresses the value of putting "first things first." Whatever system or method you use, time management is essential to decreasing your anxiety and stress at work. When you manage your time, you're actually managing *yourself*—you use time to develop strong relationships that enrich your work while still allowing you to enjoy spontaneity and meet your goals. Covey explains that we spend most of our time in one of four areas:

1. **Urgent, important** activities such as crises, pressing problems, and deadline-driven projects
2. **Not urgent, important** activities such as prevention, relationship building, planning, and recognizing new opportunities
3. **Urgent, not important** activities such as interruptions, some phone calls, some mail and reports, some meetings, pressing matters, and popular activities
4. **Not urgent, not important** activities such as trivia, busywork, some mail and calls, time wasters, and personal activities

Covey goes on to say that "first things first" does not mean everything is put into area 1 without *prioritizing* first. Constantly working in area 1 can only lead to stress and burnout. Rather, effective people shrink area 1 down to size by spending more time in area 2 and trying to stay out of areas 3 and 4.

Develop *No* Power, Not No Power

When Nike came up with their famous slogan "Just do it," bosses everywhere adopted it as their mantra for efficient management. You became expected to say yes and "just do" your job without any quibble—increasing your "busy" and losing your balance along the way.

You must learn to say no when you have too much on your plate already and the request is not mandatory. Say it pleasantly, unapologetically, and with a smile (at least in your heart and with your tone). *No* may be the most efficient balancing word in the English language. It can save you time, enable you to focus on your priorities, and protect you from your own good-heartedness.

Expect your boss and coworkers to subtly (or not so subtly) throw roadblocks in the way of your getting balanced, less busy, and not catering to everyone's needs. They're not going to like the new and improved you because it won't serve them as well. After all, it's easier for them to justify being demanding and difficult if you're acting like a stressed-out crazy person. Your busyness alleviates them from having to do what they should. Looking the part communicates to them that you expect to be exactly this frantic.

The main reasons *no* can decrease your "busy" and rebalance work:

- It doesn't beat around the bush.
- It returns responsibility to the rightful person.
- It allows you to focus on your priorities.

There are many ways to say no with discretion.

Short and Sweet
- "I have a prior commitment."
- "I'm overextended right now."
- "Sorry, can't. Let me know how it goes."
- "I'm tempted, but I'll have to pass."

Sincerely
- "I'd really love to say yes, but I just can't."
- "I'm honored, but this is a busy time, and I won't be able to fit it in."

Complimentary
- "You're so good at that, you shouldn't have any trouble finding someone to help."
- "You know I'd never refuse you if I could help it. I am swamped right now."

Offering an Alternative

▶ "We are overcommitted now—perhaps you could hire a temp for that."

▶ "I can't do that, but I can suggest a few people who might be able to help you."

▶ "I'd love to help you with this. Which of my current projects should I delegate to another person in order to take this on?"

Don't scorn the pungent clarity of *no*; it can be your ticket to balance. Yet there are times and with certain people when saying no might get you fired. Here are some guidelines for when you *cannot* say no:

▶ If you're saying no as revenge, retribution, or payback

▶ If you can't deliver it without anger or lies

▶ If you're changing a previous agreement without an alternative

▶ If the order comes down from a higher level than usual

▶ If the deadline is flexible and/or reasonable

Delegate, Don't Equivocate

When you learn to say no, you also need to learn how to delegate. If you're going to farm out the job, do it with style. Here are some things to take into consideration when delegating:

▶ Is this person capable of doing the job?

▶ Does he clearly understand what you expect?

▶ Communicate your belief that she can do it.

▶ Get her personal guarantee that she will do it.

▶ Agree upon a deadline.
▶ Let him know you'll be following up.
▶ Let her go, provide space, but *don't* do the job for her.
▶ Give praise and rewards commensurate with results.

Get More Influence, Be an Honest Employee

You may think that honesty is a no-brainer. But honest employment goes beyond telling the truth. When you're an honest employee, you do your best to live up to the performance expectations of your job. When you operate at work in an honest way, you can let go of that nagging feeling that you should do *more*.

Instead of increasing your "busy," you can try these:

▶ Stay out of sticky situations. If your gut says it's weird, listen.
▶ Don't hide problems. Covering up takes precious time and energy.
▶ Break important news fast. Give others time to solve problems.
▶ Apologize quickly to the right people and move on.

Make a "Let-Go" List

Your to-do list is four pages, single-spaced. How long is your not-to-do list, the things you intend to let go? Jim Collins, author of *Good to Great* and *Built to Last*, advocates one of my favorite ideas—making a "stop-doing" list. Since I hold tight onto too many things, I call this my "let-go" list.

▶ Make a list of everything you need to do.
▶ Prioritize the list.

▶ Combine similar tasks by resources, staff, or geographical needs.

▶ *Eliminate* the bottom two items, or purge the list 25 percent.

Some of you are starting to panic already! OK, you can start with eliminating *one* item and work up to 25 percent. Not doing things is about prioritizing and organizing, making you more able to logically show your boss why you let go of something. If done prudently and sensibly (i.e., with delegation and work-arounds), letting go of some tasks won't jeopardize your job. You won't get fired for being a more efficient and productive employee.

Be Connectable, SOFTEN Your Image

We need armor when we're battling the competition, climbing the corporate ladder, and smashing glass ceilings. Too often the armor we adopt is a hardening of our demeanor. Sure, you are a professional and need to act like one, but have you become hard? Beware of certain words in your performance reviews that signify hardness, and listen to friends and colleagues when they comment on your behavior. The words to beware: *demanding, insensitive, tough, resistant, challenging, impervious, obtuse, stringent, inflexible, intense,* etc.

You can SOFTEN your image.

S **Smile** welcomingly. Remove your frown, unclench your jaw, and be sure to smile with your eyes, too, for sincerity's sake.

O **Open** your body language. Uncross your legs, unfold your arms, open your arms, and let them hang at your sides or rest in your lap.

F Lean **forward** slightly. Be mindful of invading personal space (18 to 24 inches).

T Reach out and **touch** someone. A brief, momentary touch on the hand or forearm does wonders for connection. Beware of touching the back or shoulder—it's condescending—and avoid the upper arm, being too close to the trunk (or a woman's breast).

E Make **eye contact**. Strike a nice balance between the weirdo solid stare and eyes wandering around their upper face.

N **Nod** slowly. Done kindly, it says, "I'm listening" or "I understand," not necessarily "I agree." (Avoid rapid nodding; it's dismissive.)

Both men and women in the workplace can benefit from making themselves more *connectable*. When you're approachable and can connect quickly with others, you'll save time and energy and keep yourself in balance.

Learn Male-Speak

The fundamental differences between the male and female brain dictate that to communicate, we need to be conscious of these distinctions. Here are the basics on how you can make contact with the men at your office and talk so they'll listen.

- **Be specific.** Ask direct questions with quantifiable nouns—who, what, where, how much, by what date. Avoid the often antagonistic *why*.
- **Focus.** Men follow conversations better if there is a focus and they know what it is. "We need to talk about our schedule for Tuesday's meeting."

▶ **Don't exaggerate or use inflammatory generalizations.** "I'm so mad I could just quit." "You never . . ." "You always . . ." "I wish just once you'd . . ."

▶ **Be brief.** Remember, shut up sooner and longer. Let him think about his answer, even if it takes a day or a week.

▶ **Summarize.** Get to the point, if you have one. Try, "This will take five minutes. . . ."

▶ **Be direct.** If you haven't noticed by now, any form of hinting will fall on deaf ears. Therefore, when making a request, ask directly: "Would you . . . ?" as opposed to "Could you . . . ?" Even after all these years with my husband, I'm still caught when I ask, "Can you take a look at my right front tire?" and Lynn smiles as he answers, "I could . . . do you want me to?"

▶ **Avoid inquiring about feelings.** Asking what a male feels rather than what he thinks is often interpreted as personal and inappropriate in the workplace.

The point is not that men and women don't communicate well, but that with the difference in brain structures and hormones, it's a wonder that they communicate at all!

Become a Digital Native

At a recent small gathering of high school chums, I was chatting with Steve Frates, who was the leader of the really-smart-kids group. He created a public policy analysis company that employs the brightest of the bright. I asked his opinion of how someone could have an advantage in today's competitive workplace; he believes that it's important to become "a digital native versus a digital immigrant. You must adopt digital technology as if you were born into it."

These days everything seems to have a computer chip in it—your phones, television, vehicle, and even your refrigerator. Being resistant to change can only hold you back in your career and your life, so you might as well embrace all the new technological advances at your fingertips. Treat yourself to that new GPS, PDA, or whatever other gadget could make your life less busy, even though the learning curve may be steep. Take it a step at a time, and soon you'll be hanging with the really smart kids!

As a digital native, you will eventually hear someone say, "It's not *if* your computer will crash, it's *when*." For all their help and time-saving capacity, gadgets with chips in them have an erratic way of giving out on you at just the wrong time. (Is there ever a good time?) Even if you have a great IT department or your favorite geek sits close by in the office, you must protect yourself.

I listen to my favorite tech guru, Leo Laporte, online and on the radio. His program has taught me so much over the years. He's always preached, "Back up, back up, back up!" Now I understand that if you don't have a backup in at least two places, you're not backed up.

I live in a small town with an old infrastructure and the odd power outages, so I have an automatic online backup, plus I use little portable drives, burn CDs, and back up to an external drive. I may be obsessive about backup, but when I spend hundreds of hours on a project, I want to balance myself by having fun with my husband or my horse, not redoing a project. Your company may have policies and procedures in place, but as extra assurance and balance, *back up for yourself.*

Find Mentors and Wise Friends

I'm always on the lookout for people to add to my "tribal elders." I can't encourage you enough to find mentors in every step of your life. During my first job as a waitress at Knott's Berry Farm, I learned speed and accuracy from the founder's daughter, Cornelia Knott. When I was a new graduate nurse, an elderly doctor who once treated Humphrey Bogart deciphered hospital politics for me. My "adopted" grandmother modeled for me the business savvy she learned from working full-time owning a non-union anchorage in San Pedro (the harbor for Los Angeles). My friend and goal buddy Luke Yankee recently sent a fan e-mail to a widely published, famous photographer. Within minutes, he heard back and was invited over for a visit at his home!

You may think that a CEO or wildly famous author wouldn't want to bother with "little ol' you," but here's a secret: It is an incredible honor when someone wants to sit at your feet and soak in your experience and knowledge. It's easier than you think, but there is an art to approaching possible mentors.

- State why you thought of contacting them: "I just read your interview in the *Wall Street Journal*."
- Give a *brief* bio of yourself: "I'm a new MBA working at ABC Industries."
- State what you admire about the person: "I admire the way you cut costs but kept jobs."
- Mention connections you have: "As an Eagle Scout like me . . ."
- Ask for a personal meeting: "I would love fifteen minutes of your time."
- Start the interview with "If you could pin down three things that have contributed to your success in _____, what would they be?"
- Let them go *on and on* about themselves—ask, "What else?" and encourage, "Go on, please."
- *Shut up* about yourself—this is about them.
- Find a way you can help them somehow.

From my interviews and stories from hundreds of students, at the end of the day they've found that usually the "higher up" (or more famous) someone is, the nicer he or she is. Believe it and dream of really *big* mentors!

Being a Road Warrior

You might think that a business trip is only a time to "get out of Dodge" and see the world, but it means much more to your company. In our digital world of teleconferences and webinars, a face-to-face meeting is often the best (or only) way to get the job done. Be aware that the costs of travel and lodging to get eyeball-to-eyeball and toe-to-toe are high, not to mention the wear and tear on you. It can be inconvenient and exhausting, but without the following, it can be a waste of time or a disaster.

▶ **Plan.** Keep a file with all papers you'll need for the trip. Confirm transportation (include alternatives). Double-check guarantees on lodging and make copies of all documents, including your boarding pass.
▶ **Location, location, location.** Request a non-connecting room away the elevator, ice machine, and vending. Give up the view or mini-suite for these if you are a light (or anxious) sleeper. After more than twenty years on the road, I know what I need for my safety and tranquility. When we travel together, my poor husband has learned to wait in the lobby until I get the room I want.
▶ **Condense.** Purge your purse for travel (wallet streamlined, key ring ridded of nonessentials, *one* check).
▶ **Consider not carrying a purse at all.** Tuck your wallet safely in a zippered briefcase compartment or business tote.

▶ **Seat bag.** A small, brightly colored zippered bag with reading glasses (or contact case), single-use eyedrops, earplugs, lip balm, mints, business cards, dollar bills, pad and pen, moisturizer, nail board, etc. The bright color ensures it isn't left behind in the plane's seatback pouch or passenger seat of the rental car.

▶ **Packing list.** Shoot for carry-on all the time. When it's a huge event, I send a box to the venue marked "Hold for Connie Merritt, Arrival (date)." Recently, while on a multicity trip, a meeting planner thought she'd help me by opening my box. Surprise! I had several books, a gift for her, and clean pjs!

▶ **ID.** Put your identification on things just like when you went to summer camp. It eliminates "Is this your charger or mine?" For my electronics, I wrap a piece of purple electrician's tape around cords—it keeps mine separate, and I can spot it when I'm packing up.

▶ **Nonperishable snacks.** Carry a health bar, breakfast bar (or cookies), apple, string cheese, nuts, pretzels, and so on in your briefcase, tote, or carry-on for flights and long drives.

▶ **Comfort.** Take some comfort items like a small down pillow, an aromatic candle in a tin, expensive mints, a DVD or two.

▶ **Nest.** When you get in your hotel room, set up your bedside table like at home (clock, book, water, flashlight, glasses, etc.). Make sure the bedding is acceptable (get the right pillow, extra blanket), hang up clothes (they'll look better), keep carry-on open on chair or rack, and put your toiletries in the bathroom.

Walking Away

There's a fine line between enduring a situation and knowing when to walk out. As Kenny Rogers sang, "You got to know when to hold 'em, know when to fold 'em, know when to walk away, and know when to run." Walking out can either mean physically leaving a meeting or quitting an unendurable job. These are points only you can answer for yourself. Nothing can take the place of your own good judgment.

Meetings

Knowing when to gracefully exit a meeting can be valuable. The following list of situations are ones in which you might be justified in walking out.

▶ The other person is not (or refuses) hearing you or you feel invisible.
▶ You're being lied to. Take note of that pit in your stomach or the alarm in your head—your BS indicator. Listen to your intuition or hunch that something's not right here. Question those points that you think are untruths.
▶ The other person is out of control. When emotions are high, communication goes down exponentially.
▶ The other person is provoking you into a fight (physically or verbally). This is the bully's favorite strategy.

Your Job

If you find it impossible to get any semblance of balance at work, it may be time for a change. Time after time, my clients have reflected back on leaving their job (sometimes even a good job!) as the best choice they ever made. What good is a high paycheck if your teenager is out of control from your lack of guidance? When was the last time your late-model car made you laugh or kept you warm on a stormy night?

How do your long hours enable you to spend time with the people who are truly important in your life? Here is how you can tell if it really is time to look for a big change:

▶ When you don't belong. When your goals or your culture or your values, beliefs, or attitudes are truly incompatible with your job.

▶ When you stay out of guilt. If you are in a position in a company that you're only staying in because you're loyal—even though you have reached the ceiling of your productivity and creativity—find another position where you can be the best person and create your highest and best self in the workplace.

▶ Does the pain of the situation outweigh the gain? You are the only one who can answer this question. Make a list of the pros and cons of your position. Also take into consideration whether the pain is temporary, transitional, or permanent.

If you're at a job that's not nourishing or productive, consider other options. Certainly every job has its upsides and downsides, but you don't need to swim upstream constantly. Take a look at it, and if it's time to move on, then walk out. But remember, it's a small world. If you must leave a position, do it with class and grace. That means make your exit plan, give plenty of notice, train your replacement if possible, say good-bye kindly to (and always speak well of) your employer and coworkers.

Part 3

Dealing with Busyness at Home

Chapter 10

Making Your Home a Sanctuary from "Busy"

Having a baby is like suddenly getting the world's worst roommate—like having Janis Joplin with a bad hangover and PMS come to stay with you.

—Anne Lamott

Wouldn't it be nice if your only task was conquering busyness at work? But many of us have second (or even third) jobs waiting when we get home from work. During my speaking engagements, I ask a simple question: "What makes you busy?" The answers have convinced me that taking control of your "busy" at home presents a new set of challenges different from those that you must face on the job. Home responsibilities as a working parent—single or married—will tip you into the "busy danger zone."

If you're trying to do it all at home, take heart! With a little planning and tweaking of your at-work strategies, you can transform your crazy busy to a *designed* busy at home. I've heard all your excuses why you can't change it.

- "I've always been this way."
- "I'm from a dysfunctional family."
- "My spouse doesn't help out."
- "My kids need to (name activity) to get into (name school)."
- "There aren't enough hours in the day."

No matter the excuse, though, your new goal should be taking the lead in making your home a sanctuary. It will take recruiting family members to organize and schedule your home to get you out of the "busy danger zone."

Round Up the Troops

The best way to make a change at your home is to set realistic goals. Is your household in chaos? Shoot for ordered messiness. You don't have to be a dictator, killjoy, or tyrant to craft a less busy, more peaceful home. Begin with a mandatory household meeting—all household members, including your partner, housemates, children, and boarders. Tell everyone something that they'd like to hear: "We're going to have a family meeting so that our lives will start to be more fun." It's mandatory attendance, not optional. Don't worry if you get lots of sighs, gripes, and eye rolling. Your attitude here should be "too bad, we're having the meeting anyway."

This meeting can be the start of you getting some help from your family. Tell them why you need their help—your busyness around the house is starting to take its toll in a major way—but if everyone pitches in, it won't be so bad. Promise them that the changes you ask for have one goal in mind—a happier home. You're on your way to undoing months (or years) of busyness damage and creating a sanctuary for yourself and every family member.

Sacred Schedules

Another order of business for a family meeting is for each person to map out his or her schedule for the next six months (or year). This is important to do because you'll not only be giving each person a voice in the family, but also teaching them valuable life skills. Each person needs to list every important, save-the-day event coming up, as well as all the regularly scheduled activities. You and your mate know your holidays, vacations, and mandatory attendance activities. Every child's school has a master calendar. Don't forget to produce everyone's sports schedules. (Soccer can monopolize so much time that some of my friends have admitted to praying that their kid's team *doesn't* get into the finals!)

Each person will make his or her own weekly schedule, Sunday through Saturday. Include all the details that are part of each family member's separate daily routine:

▶ Wake-up time, morning meal
▶ Leave for school, job, activity
▶ After-school activities
▶ Evening mealtime
▶ Homework, office work
▶ Free time
▶ Bedtime

After individual schedules are made, get everyone on the same page, literally. Post a master calendar in the kitchen so each family member gets a better view (and sense) of working together as a team. It also gives everyone a dose of reality—how much time you actually do or don't have. You'll see how fairly you're dividing your time between family members, your job, commitments, and yourself. Other family members will discover that they are receiving their fair share of family resources and attention. Most families post a paper or dry-erase month-at-a-look calendar with large boxes for each day. It's best when only one person writes on it—others can make requests (with stick-on notes or verbally), but this keeps it honest. Keep different-colored pens on a string for nearby use. Here is how it should be filled out:

▶ Activities involving everyone are written in black.
▶ Note birthdays, anniversaries, and special days.
▶ Mark holidays.
▶ Add scheduled vacations with leave-the-house times (i.e., "4:30 A.M. leave for airport," not "Flight at 8:30 A.M.").

▶ Each member has a specific color for his or her activities.

▶ Note scheduled doctor appointments and professional visits.

▶ Note after-school or extracurricular activities and times.

▶ Note all save-the-date appointments.

▶ Times are posted to include departure and arrival times. That is, "4:15–6:15 Yoga" includes fifteen minutes for travel time each way for a 4:30 to 5:30 lesson plus a half hour for your grocery run.

▶ Put parentheses around any posting that is tentative or unconfirmed.

▶ Erase parentheses when it's permanent.

You may already do this and have it all plugged into your handheld, but once it's up there for the whole family to see, they'll better understand your methods. (They might even learn when they can and cannot push you.) Print out the calendar and evaluate what needs to be curbed, altered, or *eliminated*.

Family members will learn to piggyback on each other's activities, saving not only time but also money on gas and with multiple-user discounts. They will start self-regulating and managing their own time when they realize that in order to pursue a new interest, they must give up another. Everyone will choose those activities that align with goals and time available.

Unleash Your Inner Bitch

I believe that we've been afraid of our inner bitch for too long. In the literal sense, a bitch is a female canine that does not yield to scorn from her challengers—she'll stand her ground until they back down, especially when protecting her pups. If your "busy" is out of control at home, it's time to flaunt your healthy inner bitch. I know, you've probably already tried barking and snapping at your family or housemates. The problem with this is they all know they just have to outlast you or ignore you and you'll back down, give up, and go away. It's time to be consistent—set your house rules and stand your ground.

Implementing big changes in the structure and regulation of your household might seem so, well, military. But I've found one consistent thread of long-lasting marriages and families that are inoculated against chaos in the midst of crazy busyness—they are *vigilant watchdogs* of their values and standards. In rough economic times or during health challenges, they had *rules*, which everyone could rely on to be consistent. You want your home to be a touchstone of consistency upon which all family members can trust, rely, and receive comfort.

The pups (family members) may rebel at first, but display your healthy inner bitch and stand your ground for the new house rules.

Family Time

The inner bitch sets a regular time that is absolutely positively no-excuses family time without interruption, meaning zero distractions—phone ringers off, no TV, no texting, no earbuds. Make consequences for absence or infractions, such as losing a privilege or financial penalty. Start with the same night each week and work up to more. Most families start with "family dinner night." Communication and connection come "in the spaces" during offhand questions, brief comments, and silences. You may be chewing in silence with sullen teenagers, but stick to it, you're building a tradition. You're building something valuable— a running dialog. Create those spaces, because communicating *now* means less acting out *to be heard* later. To the inner bitch, family time saves time, energy, and busyness in the future.

Feeding Time

The inner bitch makes meal shopping routine and meal prep possible for everyone. Teach all family members how to nourish themselves quickly without a drive-through. Start by having a whiteboard on the fridge with the week's menu and prep assignments posted. In the beginning, you will have to be the diet dictator until the family starts taking initiative and responsibility. For example, the whole chicken can be washed, seasoned, and put in the oven by a teen; the frozen veggies can be microwaved by a preteen; the rice directions can be followed by your mate; and even a young child can concoct a dessert with flavored yogurt and fruit. In the summer, you can teach everyone the basics of grilling, and wintertime is perfect for an everything-but-the-kitchen-sink soup in the slow cooker.

Assign each family member to plan a dinner each week. Post the weekly shopping list. Tell everyone that if it's not on the list, it doesn't get bought, including toilet paper, toothpaste, and tampons. Teach everyone how to shop and follow the list. Not only can this list save money on impulse buying, but it can also cut down on the need for frequent grocery store trips and fast food. Just think how much your busyness will be decreased when you're not the only person in charge of meal planning, shopping, and preparation.

Online Time

Harness your inner bitch by instituting rules that include surfing the Internet, gaming, instant messaging, e-mailing, and social networking, whether on a desktop, laptop, or handheld device. House rules apply to everyone, and some examples are "no electronics during meals," "black screens from 10 P.M. to 6 A.M.," or "thirty-minute shopping sessions." You can waste so much time electronically tethered that your home tasks take longer, you don't get enough sleep, wake up groggy, and make hurrying out the door the norm. Is it any wonder you start your day rushed and busy? When you and your mate follow these rules, your kids will benefit in many ways—you will be modeling good behavior and saving the next generation from the "busy danger zone."

TV Time

We buy these complicated surround-sound, large-screen home theater systems, and they become the centerpiece of our homes. With digital recorders, we can even zoom through the commercials (except for the ones with a cute puppy). But do we really have to watch reruns of "Two and a Half Men" every night and have the nightly news as background noise for dinner? Turn off the tube! Nielsen Media Research reports individual television viewing in our nation is more than four hours a day. That is equivalent to a part-time job! Besides wasting time, watching television is sedentary and brain deadening—leading to a plethora of health troubles from obesity and diabetes to attention and cognitive problems.

Watching too much television is a lot like smoking; people know the side effects and do it anyway. Let your inner bitch regulate television.

▶ Make rules for hours of operation. It can't be the background soundtrack for your home life!
▶ Trade no-television time for other activities. Take a walk after dinner instead.

▶ Use viewing time to barter with the kids. Read for sixty minutes for thirty minutes of TV.
▶ Leverage viewing time as a reward for chores done by teens and children.
▶ Make family night at the movies an event. Get a brand-new DVD that everyone can agree on, prepare some movie munchies, and have fun.

Quiet Time

Your inner bitch makes no excuses for her need for privacy and solitude. The home should be the place where each family member can recharge his or her batteries—especially you. Institute the four Rs for quiet time:

▶ Pick a **regular** time when you are not to be disturbed—except for emergencies involving bodily damage or fire.
▶ **Reinforce** your rule. Make consequences for interruptions, such as losing a privilege.
▶ **Respect** others' quiet time. Give them time to reestablish their own equilibrium.
▶ **Reward** them for respecting your quiet time. Emerge from your private time a more pleasant and refreshed person.

Often you think you need a week's sleep when all you need is a long bath with some quiet in the house. A quick recharging of the batteries ensures you'll be much more present for the rest of the night.

Delegating Chores and Housekeeping

Cleanliness may be next to godliness, but spotlessness is next to craziness. Some of the loudest applause I receive is when I tell an all-female group, "Divide and conquer your housekeeping!" I stress that the goal is to give up on the dream of a spotless home without letting the place go to seed. If you're single and living alone, look to lowering your standards of what you call "clean." I can't tell you how *freeing* it was when I gave myself permission to *not* have a spotless home.

Each family member can contribute to the efficient running of your home. The first step to make in doling out chores is to make a list. Go around your house and make an assessment. Then list all the chores and housekeeping in your home that will make it livable. (Remember—it doesn't need to be perfect!) Now it's up to you to figure out which chores to delegate to whom. Enforce that this is not voluntary; it's part of what it means to be a family member.

- ▶ **Cleaning.** Make each person responsible to declutter and clean his or her own bedroom and bath. The common areas, such as kitchen, hallways, and family rooms, can be divvied up by week according to ability. Heavy cleaning, such as for windows, screens, and blinds, should be done together on a weekend morning.
- ▶ **Meal prep.** Believe it or not, this is something everyone can pitch in to do. (See "Feeding Time" earlier in this chapter.)
- ▶ **Laundry.** Working mothers should not automatically be the ones doing laundry for the entire house. Each person can be taught how to wash, fold, and put away his or her clothes and change the sheets on the bed. For young children, you can encourage them by telling them this is the way "big kids" do it.
- ▶ **Pets.** Who feeds, exercises, and cleans up after Fido? Is the cat avoiding the litter box on purpose? The feeding and cleaning up of the family pet is rotated among

all family members. If a child has her own small pet (hamster, fish, snake, lizard) in her room, she must feed and clean up after it.

Listmania

Become a list maker. My friends laugh at the lists I have for *everything*. Oh, sure, I am a bit obsessive, but I've never been without my toothbrush when trapped in an airport or without my husband's size when I find 501s on sale. Here are a few of my favorite and indispensable lists.

▶ **People lists.** I use ACT!, a contact management software, on my computer. It has lots of basic fields, including name, address, e-mail, phones, and website, along with blank ones that I use for birthdays, anniversaries, and preferences. I code and group everyone according to where they fit (friends, family, church, clients, readers, organizations, media, etc.). It's a drag to set up, but a lifesaver for labels, holiday cards, targeted mailings, etc.

▶ **Goals.** Writing your goals on paper not only gives you a chance to dream wonderful things for yourself, it invokes powers *unseen* to work on your behalf. I have been formally and intentionally writing my goals since I was in high school and can attest that this works.

▶ **Packing lists.** Have one ready for every type of travel you embark on. Make your lists detailed right on down to your specific toiletries, electronics (especially chargers), and underwear. This is especially needed if you do "carry-on only" for business trips. My packing lists include "Business Travel," "Tropical Travel," "Cold Weather Personal," "Travel with Husband and Dog," "Day Trail (on horse)," and "Overnight with Horse" (like moving a condo!).

Shopping Lists

I've noticed that when I go shopping without my list I forget items and spend more money than I should. Without my list, I can't remember if we need tomatoes, so I buy some; but if it turns out I had them already, now we have so many that they end up rotting. I often get distracted by some free sample and buy it on impulse.

Keep the household lists posted so everyone participates and learns to be a better shopper.

▶ **Groceries.** Weekly shopping for meals and supplies becomes faster and cheaper (no impulse buying) when you include brand, size, and general price.

▶ **Big box.** Bulk items at the warehouse stores can save bundles, but if you leave it up to impulse shopping, you might get lost in the massive aisles, debating whether to purchase that year's worth of Heath bars that's on sale.

▶ **Items for delivery.** You can save so much time when you don't have to drive and park. Bulk buy your supplies for office or home business, school, projects, and pets from a list so you can take advantage of sales and free or reduced delivery fees for orders (usually offered for purchases over $50).

▶ **Clothes.** You'll save oodles of time (and untold dollars) when you keep a running clothes list. Organize it by person and occasion, favorite brands and sizes such as "Lisa: underwear, CK, ~~brief,~~ medium," or "David: dress-up, navy blazer, 40 long." Keep it handy in your calendar (electronic or paper), crossing off and reprinting as needed. Watch for holiday sales, seasonal specials, rebates, and twofers.

The Great Purge

Another big part of your new organizational initiative, and the second order of business during your family meeting, is getting your home in order by purging your unnecessary stuff. Dividing up chores will only help so much if your house is overstuffed to begin with. More important than your workspace, your home needs to be an oasis of order and space. A cleaning of this magnitude may seem like more trouble than it's worth, but by freeing your home from clutter, you will save time in the long run. You must be ruthless about "the Purge": if you haven't touched, worn, read, played with, or used it in the past nine months—toss it! This is not mere reorganizing, but de-busifying. Organizing is rearranging current piles in a new way; de-busifying is getting rid of stuff so you'll never have to organize it.

Set a deadline for when each person will go through all of his or her personal *stuff*—clothes, books, toiletries, toys. Let them know that if they don't do this, you will do it for them—and they *don't* want that! Set a date that all of you will go through the garage, storage areas, and basement. Don't forget the kitchen and pantry—surely there are items that you've never gotten around to cooking with and never will. Donating nonperishable items to a local food bank not only is good for your space, it's good for your community.

Load up on large garbage bags and used boxes, and get ready to do some tossing! You should have three distinct destinations for everything you will no longer need:

▶ **Sell** items that have some value in a garage sale, online auction, or consignment store. Make sure the price you're asking justifies your time and effort; if not, you might feel better about donating certain items, even if they are fairly nice or new.

▶ **Give away** items that have no value to sell but are still usable to someone.
▶ **Trash** anything broken, damaged, junky, or threadbare.

Exceptions can be antiques, heirlooms, and high-value memorabilia—*not* all the piddly ones. Olympic medal (yes), all 83 soccer trophies (no).

Once you know what you have to get rid of, put items on online auction. With a little research, you can discover which items are ideal for selling online; it varies and is always surprising. (I've sold an antique stove, custom saddle, and goofy souvenirs.) Set a day for your garage sale, and anything not sold online within a week will be put up for the garage sale. Whatever items you can't sell then should just be tossed out or taken to charity with the giveaway items. All profits should go into a special fund to provide some relief for the family or to reward everyone for a good job. A friend of mine earned so much from her "purge" that she settled a debt that was looming over her. (She had a *lot* of stuff.)

Making the Purge Permanent

When Lyle and Donna married late in life, they merged their households and downsized to a small condo in a beautiful location. Once there, they discovered they had two or three of many of their appliances, plus a bunch of stuff they forgot they even owned. The move accomplished a purge on its own, but they were in danger of reverting to their old pack rat ways. They both agreed to an in-out rule—whenever you bring in something new, you must take out the item it replaced. They found that if they didn't want to get rid of the old one, it was probably not a good idea to buy a new one. As a result, they kept clutter down to a minimum and spent their money on traveling to exotic places.

You will stay less busy if you keep your commitment to reevaluating everything you buy, right on down to the souvenirs and tchotchkes you pick up on vacation. (Those shell leis are fun, but do they go with anything besides your pareo on vacation?) I promise you when you institute the in-out rule, your home and life will stay uncluttered and peaceful.

No Eulogies for the Death of "Busy"

Making your home a sanctuary is one of the greatest gifts you can give your family and yourself. You'll need courage and conviction to institute some new (and often tough) house rules, but you will be thrilled with the refuge your home provides for you and the whole family. Once you live in a home that is a safe haven from "busy," you'll want to tell the world! Be careful when you're tempted to tell your too-busy friend that she should have a family meeting and release her inner bitch! Fight the urge to preach or teach. Don't eulogize your process or try to convert other busy people to your family's new way of being. Just let them wonder why you're so happy all of a sudden.

Chapter 11

Getting De-Stressed at Home

Any woman who understands the problems of running a home will be nearer to understanding the problems of running a country.

—Margaret Thatcher

W hich came first: stress at work or stress at home? These two conditions are almost always inter-related. Chances are that if you're stressed in one place, the baggage spills into other areas of your life. When you're always busy and stressed at work and at home, you develop a "stress lifestyle." Stress becomes more than something you just experience, it becomes the way you lead your life. You must break this cycle—not only to preserve your sanity and maintain your physical health but also to increase your enjoyment of life.

Check Your "Duh" Factors

Just like at work, when you get home, there are probably stressors staring you right in the face. You get so accustomed to certain routines day in and day out that you don't even notice how worn down they tend to leave you. Take a look around your home and you'll see some obvious changes you can make that will cut your stress by a percentage. And in the stress-reduction business, every little bit helps—heck, it might be enough to keep you out of the "busy danger zone."

▶ **Your sounds.** Some sounds can cause stress (noisy neighbors, noisy kids), and some sounds can be soothing (down-tempo jazz, silence). If you're greeted

190

with the wrong sounds when you get home, it's time to take a stand and reclaim your auditory space.

▶ **Your exercise.** Certainly raising kids and running a home is physical work, but just because you're tired doesn't mean you've gotten your workout in for the day during your commute. To support your body in fighting stress, you need to get your heart rate up (aerobic exercise) two to three times a week, along with gently stretching your muscles and joints daily.

▶ **Your self-medication.** If you use drugs, alcohol, or junk food to relieve your tension, you may be masking or creating symptoms that need professional attention. Get a physical checkup with the basics—blood pressure, blood work, and urinalysis.

▶ **Your sleeping area.** Not getting enough rest is both a symptom of and a cause for more stress throughout the day. If you aren't getting your eight hours in, then you should do a "sleep check" to evaluate the hours you spend in bed—your mattress quality, your blankets and pillows, as well as the room temperature, humidity, darkness, and noise factors.

▶ **Your accessibility.** Can anyone contact you at any time? Turn your cell phone and BlackBerry ringers and alarms off before bedtime, use caller ID to screen, get off call lists, and move your fax machine where you won't be disturbed by incoming transmissions.

▶ **Your smells.** Pollutants such as smoke, traffic, and animal dander can add to stress. Use air purifiers, fans, and anti-allergen sprays to counteract those stress-producing odors and impurities.

▶ **Your taxi service.** Are you ferrying everyone around everywhere? Explore the option of sharing carpooling duties, utilizing public transportation, or combining errands with dropping the kids off for lacrosse practice.

▶ **Your duties.** If you've complained that you're the only one doing household chores, divide shopping, cleaning, and laundry among family members.

Let's look at ten steps I recommend to get dramatic results from your efforts to eliminate stress at home.

Get Moving

Exercise is one of the most potent antidotes to stress. Everyone knows that in theory, if not in practice. The main reason is that it decreases cortisol, a main stress hormone in your body, and increases endorphins, your "feel good" chemicals. Besides giving you a healthy glow, exercise can also provide a distraction to take your mind off your problems along with strengthening your immune system. If these aren't reasons enough, research suggests that by lowering your physiological reactivity to stress *today*, exercise may give you some immunity to *future* stress.

Your job outside the home may be physically demanding, and perhaps the thought of being *more* physical at home is enough to stress you out. But to receive nature's stress-busters, endorphins, you need to get your heart rate up three times a week for at least twenty minutes. Experts disagree somewhat on the rate, length, and frequency of exercise, but they all agree that you have to get out there and do it.

To start your regimen, begin with simple activities such as taking a brisk walk. The key to getting enough exercise to de-stress is to make it a priority. Do not wait until the end of the day to exercise, when you may not feel like it. Most people report that getting up one half hour earlier and getting their exercise out of the way first thing in the morning creates a positive spin to their day. Figure out which part of your day is better for working out and make it a part of your routine *today*.

▶ **Turn chores into games.** Put on music and boogie as you do your cleaning, give yourself a reward if you "win" (get it done) within a certain time, or go for your personal best time for cleaning and organizing.

▶ **Learn a new sport or take a class.** When you've got that beginner's excitement, it doesn't feel so much like exercise with a capital E. There are many different sports and classes that working parents can fit in their schedule. You can set up activities parallel to your children's schedules, such as learning tai chi when they are at karate or shooting hoops during their basketball teams' practices. The whole family could join a race team for a charity walk/run, go to the batting cages, or take lessons in golf, scuba diving, horseback riding, or kayaking.

You can also de-stress your body through repetitive activities. Dr. Herbert Benson of Harvard Medical School has confirmed the benefits of the "relaxation response" since the late seventies. These activities include walking, playing a musical instrument, knitting, and any other hobby that doesn't take serious concentration. Repetition can bring you a state of mental calm that lowers your blood pressure and releases tension.

Get Properly Nourished

A stressed body is a demanding machine that needs the proper balance of fluids, vitamins, minerals, and nutrients. Unfortunately, we sometimes eat what makes us feel better—that's why it's called comfort food—or try some new supplement because it promises quick results. The straight scoop on nutrition *does not* come from a celebrity, infomercial spokesperson, or pills. The truth will come from science—research, double-blind studies, and peer reviews—not stories, advertising, and sound bites. Proper nourishment requires that you make an effort to do the following:

▶ Be skeptical of miracle supplements sold online or on television—"Lose a pound a day without diet or exercise!"

▶ Look to the real story behind sensational headlines like "Miracle Juice Curbs Appetite!"

▶ Consult a registered dietician (R.D.) or your doctor before you start a weight-loss program.

▶ Watch sweet and salty foods, because high intakes of sugar can lead to diabetes, and salt affects heart health.

▶ Slow down and enjoy meals instead of eating on the go. If you eat slower, your appetite will be satisfied faster and you'll consume less and experience fewer mood swings from blood sugar rushes.

▶ Monitor your alcohol intake, because it can suppress your appetite for the nutrition you actually *need*, and alcohol abuse, whether chronic or episodes of binge drinking, can suppress immune function.

Get a Pet (or Play More with Yours)

Pets can help your mental state by making you laugh, distracting your negative thoughts, and giving you unconditional love. Petting a cat or dog actually helps you physiologically by lowering your heart rate and blood pressure. They also will get you out of the house. Many couples use the pet-walking time to wind down their day and reconnect with each other. Try it with your kids. I know they'll say it's lame, but make it more fun to go on a walk than sit in front of the tube: "Rex and I are walking downtown to get ice cream," or "I'm taking Muffie to meet her new boyfriend at the dog park."

Make sure you make decisions beforehand about who is in charge of caring for, feeding, and exercising the new addition to the family. One of my hyper-stressed clients ferried her son to the pet store three times a week for the live crickets his "designer lizard" needed. I suggested she make him responsible for getting the live food for this creature. I challenged her to make her son solve the problem—get the crickets yourself or sell Godzilla. Guess what? He found them online, and they are now delivered directly to the door!

Get Happy

It used to be that only the New Age thinkers or "those crazy hippies" believed that your thoughts could actually influence your health. Medical research increasingly supports the mind-body connection. Evidence from the field of psychoneuroimmunology gives us positive proof of the connection between our thoughts and our health. The easiest way to get happy in a hurry is to remember not to take life so seriously. When stuff happens, you have to learn to let it roll off your back. Meticulous researchers Rick Foster and Greg Hicks recount in their book *Choosing Brilliant Health* how you can learn to create positive emotions by using positive words instead of negative ones (e.g., saying "I am calm" instead of "I will not be stressed"). Here are some other ways to improve your attitude at home:

▶ **Transcendental meditation.** This technique involves intense breathing exercises and repetitions of words. Dr. Robert Schneider, principal author of a research study conducted at five universities and medical centers, tracked 202 patients with high blood pressure for up to eighteen years. It was reported that those practicing transcendental meditation for twenty minutes twice daily had a 23 percent lower death rate from all causes and nearly a one-third lower death rate from heart disease than those not practicing meditation. Locate classes online or at a holistic health center.

▶ **Deep breathing or pranayama.** *Pranayama* is a technical term in yoga that means lengthening or controlling breath or *prana*. Inhale, relaxing your abdomen, pushing your belly forward and expanding it. Exhale, allowing your abdomen to shrink back in, tighten your belly muscles, and push the air out. Inhale the same length of time that you exhale. Breathing serves as the pump for your lymphatic system, carrying away the detritus of your immune system and toxins—a drainage system throughout the body.

▶ **Guided imagery.** This is a method of meditation and breathing where you use your mind to create images— like a vivid daydream—to communicate positive messages to your whole body or the parts you choose. First popularized by cancer patients, guided imagery classes can be found at most medical and wellness centers, or you can find instruction online, from a CD, or from a therapist.

Get Down

The biochemicals your body generates throughout the day as you deal with your busy life can end up keeping you awake at night. Your habits and patterns directly impact your ability to get the necessary stress relief from a good night's sleep. It's normal to have occasional bouts of insomnia the nights before a big, important day. The problem comes when your insomnia-stress cycle becomes chronic. Here are some ways to avoid this fate:

▶ **Practice "sleep hygiene,"** a bedtime *routine* in which sleep is the last step. Your body will love the consistency and rhythm of a wind-down from your day. This routine may or may not include the following activities: setting out your morning clothes; showering;

applying body lotion; getting your jammies on; setting the alarm; getting into bed; five to ten minutes of positive, grateful thoughts or prayers; reading for fifteen minutes; putting earplugs in; and turning out the light.

▶ **Buy a new mattress.** Don't even try to get a bargain on a mattress; you can't comparison shop, because every store has a different line. You know it's the right mattress when you get a deep sleep and wake up without aches and pains. Choose one with your partner, buy it with a guarantee, have it delivered, and give it a test run for thirty days.

▶ **Check your cushions, pillows, and blankets.** When your body is responding to allergens, it produces histamines that interfere with restorative sleep, so look for offensive materials (feathers, wool, synthetics) and remove them from your sleep zone.

▶ **Eliminate your sleep disrupters.** Identify the culprit interrupting your sleep, whether it's noise or light or whatever, and find a buffer or solution. Use white-noise machines, eye masks, or earplugs. On hot summer nights, my squishy, foam earplugs allow me to get fresh breezes from open windows while blocking out our neighbors' noisy activities.

Get Touched

Human contact is a deep physical and emotional need. A good way to unwind at the end of the day or the end of the week is with some kind of touching activity with another person. Nothing melts stress away like a good rubdown!

▶ **Massage.** A licensed massage therapist can interrupt the neurohormones connected with stress. If the local spa is too pricey, try a massage school. Or draft your mate to be your personal masseuse.

▶ **Acupuncture.** This is not a quick fix, but if pain is keeping you from sleep, six to eight sessions may give you some relief.

▶ **Sex with someone you love.** This is one of the greatest stress relievers known to mankind.

Get Laughing

Cultivating humor is a healthier practice than you might suspect. It can relieve you of stress, support your immune system, and even increase your endurance. Besides providing a physical and emotional release, laughter reduces stress hormones and increases endorphins. A deep belly laugh exercises your diaphragm, abs, and even your heart. When you're laughing, you're getting a distraction away from negative emotions and lightening your perspective on your troubles. Get more giggles:

▶ **Hang around fun people.** Laughter, fun, and good times are increased around funny people and those who have a lighter view of the world.

▶ **Rent comedy DVDs.** Even if you rent the same ones over and over rather than checking out new releases, it's hard to beat a solid comedy. Everyone has a movie or particular series that never fails to tickle the funny bone.

▶ **Go to comedy clubs.** Live comedy makes humor contagious; you'll laugh sooner and longer when everyone else around you is laughing.

▶ **Keep a laugh journal of funny things.** Look for humor in your frustrations; you'll be training yourself to "look back and laugh about it" *now*. Collect funny jokes, cartoons, and sayings and go through the file when you're feeling stressed or down.

Get Clear on Any Lingering Problems

If your home is to be stress-free, then it's important to clear the air whenever there is friction (and no matter what, there will be friction sometimes). You must learn to defuse flare-ups of sibling rivalry and other conflicts as they arise if you're ever going to move forward in the right direction.

Take a Deep Breath and Shut Up

Most of us tend to respond *immediately* during conflicts, based on our perspective. Try not responding—at least not with words. A friend could raise one eyebrow without another facial movement; it said so much with so little and allowed her to keep her cool. She told me that it gave her a signal to *not* respond when things were hitting the fan— and the chance for a time-out to regroup her emotions. Remember, less can often be more. Next time you feel an urge to respond, fix it, or fight back . . . take a deep breath, let it out slowly, look thoughtful, and see what happens.

Call a Time-Out in Family Tiffs

In nearly every sport, a coach can call time-out, usually to realign a strategy or because a player is injured. You're the "coach" in your family, so when family arguments make you (and your "team") highly emotional, scattered, or stressed, ask for a time-out. Give everyone a breather by say-ing, "I think we're in gridlock and need some time to cool off. Let's give it a rest and discuss this tomorrow morning at ten." This can help you and your family members look at the situation without high drama or strong emotions cloud-ing your judgment. The final outcome may change toward the positive when you get the composure and perspective afforded by a cooldown. Sometimes the anger dissipates, and apologies are given and received.

Get New Friends

We are raised from the beginning to be winners and to accumulate stuff, and sometimes that aspect of our life becomes our entire life. One of the most important parts of life—making it truly worth living—is being with good friends. It is a necessary part of a healthy life and a sure way to de-stress, as well. If you're feeling pinned down by the demands of your job and your home life, perhaps that's a signal that you need some new friends in your life or to spend some time with the ones you've already got. Make connections with people who are open, accepting, warm, and who genuinely like you. Connect more with people you admire and want to be like.

We All Need Support

Build your support system by connecting with friends and family who are your cheerleaders. Spend time with them for no good reason other than hanging out and watching the world go by. Those people you invest love in will pay you huge dividends when you need them the most. Connecting is important to your health and life. Scientific research reveals that excessive isolation can lead to a weakening of the immune system, serious diseases, and even premature death!

Don't Take On Others' Problems

It's important to be there for your friends when they need you, but equally as important that you don't solve their problems for them. Think of your friends asking you for help with their problems as if they are tossing you a skunk.

You wouldn't hang onto a skunk, would you? You'd try to get rid of it! When they try to enlist you to solve their problems, empower them to take on the challenge by asking *them* for a solution. You might ask, "What would you like to see happen in this situation?" Or ask, "What would you feel is a fair outcome?" Toss the skunk back to them—solving their problems just stinks!

Get Down with the Power Up There

Stress relief often comes from a force that is beyond time and the material world—your spirituality. When you choose to nurture your spirituality, you'll be tapping into stress relief that is difficult to explain, much less quantify. It may be rooted in a particular religious practice or simply a belief in a higher power. Open yourself to a metaphysical reality greater than what you can identify through your senses— you may receive stress relief from mighty surprising forces.

Anchor to Your Higher Power

One of the best vacations I've experienced was when I joined several friends in chartering sailboats in the Caribbean. One beautiful afternoon, a sudden storm transformed our stress-free vacation into a serious struggle. The metal line holding up the boat's mainsail snapped, bringing the sail and its heavy boom crashing into the cockpit. Radioing for help, we were told to start the engine, drag our anchor, and head directly into the wind. I also put out my own personal anchor—prayer—and asked for strength and hope from a power greater than myself. After the storm cleared, we found a calm cove to do the necessary repairs. When you're in troubled waters, get your engine started, head into the trouble, and keep your "anchor" out. Soon you will find yourself in a tranquil cove.

Meet with Other Spiritually Inclined Friends

More than two decades ago, I attended a large church that encouraged the power of small groups. Our multi-thousand-member congregation was broken up into smaller geographic groups that could meet bimonthly closer to home. Our "minichurch" evolved into a small (ten to sixteen people), informal, flexible group of people with a wide range of age, experience, education, and spiritual path. Over the years, we've faced the joys and sorrows of life together with a level of strength and support that can't be described. But beyond being a soft place to fall, my "minichurch" folks have become family and a rock-solid foundation for my spiritual life, which has helped my stress level immensely.

Your At-Home Commitments

Your ability to de-stress your home is directly proportional to how determined you are to stay out of the "busy danger zone." Commit right now to eliminate your at-home stress by checking your "Duh" factors and using a couple (or all) of the ten steps in this chapter. Complete your plan:

The one action I will take this week is _____.
Within two weeks, I will _____.
Within one month, I will _____.
In six months, my home will be _____.

Congratulations! You're on the way to making your home a stress-free zone. Best of all, you're creating a place of peace and contentment not only for yourself but your whole family. Once you start to see the little things you can do to alleviate the day-to-day stressors from your life, you'll get used to practicing them automatically.

Chapter 12

Putting Balance
Back into
Your Life

*You are the only person alive who
has sole custody of your life.*

—Anna Quindlen

M any things in life are difficult, but the *impossible* just takes a little more time and planning. You're looking for balance that will allow you to make sense of your busy life. I used to believe that it would be impossible to balance my life. The months (and years) leading up to my collapse from being overbusy had me in the middle of a five-ring circus—family, friends, work, play, and study. By the time I woke up to the crazy busyness that had my life so out of balance, I probably had fried many brain cells, clogged numerous vessels, and taxed some of my organs to *just this close* to failing. But that's when I managed to do something about it. Life may be difficult, but putting balance into it just takes a little more time and planning. This chapter will explore making it possible through

- ▶ Balancing work
- ▶ Staying healthy
- ▶ Other people in your life
- ▶ Your master plan

When you choose to balance your life, it has to be on your own terms. *What is balance to you?* No one else's definition matters. You need a very clear idea of what you want;

it's not enough to say what you *don't* want. Defining your balance means taking an intense look at each area of your life and articulating what your life would look like if every individual part were in order.

It takes courage to scrutinize the choices and actions that have led up to where you are now. It takes a lot of guts to change habits, admit mistakes, right the wrongs, and let go of non-nourishing relationships and live a less busy, more contented life. But your busyness isn't going to naturally sort itself out. It's up to you to do the heavy lifting.

Our society and pervasive media exert great pressure on us to have it all. My survey respondents have serious concerns about their ability to balance the demands of jobs and families. Even without a family, the art of balancing your work and home life is critical. When you're out of balance, worry, fear, anxiety, and stress will destroy the contentment and peace that you deserve.

Orphanages in England during World War II saw an understandably high amount of nightmares, agitation, and anxious crying. A nightly practice was instituted of giving each child a piece of bread to hold with the instruction that he or she could eat it in the morning. The nightmares and other anxious behaviors decreased. It was surmised that the children's uncertain future was quelled by their trust that they would have their bread in the morning.

Begin to discover your "piece of bread," your security, by keeping track of your activities for a week. And I do mean all of your activities. Television watching, helping your son with homework, reading magazines—everything. This assessment will help you to identify what's *truly* necessary, what you enjoy most, and what satisfies you. Really examine the time you spend away from work and look toward creating a place that you can trust will rebalance and lead you to a life less busy.

Balancing Work into Your Life (and Not Life into Your Work)

The first time I had a garbage disposal jam, I smacked my forehead when the plumber walked in, pressed the little red button on the bottom, and handed me a bill for his house call. A jammed, overbusy life is your signal to hit your reset button. The first step to this process is to balance making a living into living.

Keeping Work at Work

It's no simple task to leave work at work. It's hard to break focus from an activity that is critical to your finances and consumes the majority of your waking hours—getting ready, getting there, getting it done, and getting home. Take control of this situation by giving yourself time to do the things that are most important to you. It's always possible to find more time for your family and your hobbies, no matter how hectic things seem at the office. Here are some suggestions that can help you lead a more rewarding personal life once you're off the clock:

- ▶ **Find options for work hours.** Explore flextime, a compressed workweek, job sharing, or telecommuting. Changing your work routine can free up hours at home *and* lift your spirits.
- ▶ **Fight the guilt.** It's OK to have a life outside of work (for both men and women) even though your company culture may not agree. Trust that if you do a good job and you get there on time, it's hard for the company to argue with your need to have a life outside of work.
- ▶ **Plan tomorrow.** Before you leave work, make a plan for tomorrow's projects and activities. Knowing where

you need to start helps to disengage from work mode and not be overwhelmed when you return.

▶ **Take a regular train home.** When you have frequent departure options, don't be tempted to work "just a little longer" because you think you can always catch a later train. Small infringements on personal time add up to big insults to your family and your balance.

▶ **Have a "wind-down" routine.** Use commute time to start relaxing. Picture a little stress lifting with each step (or mile). Imagine your concerns and worries floating away until they are gone when you walk in the door.

▶ **Cut your e-leash when you get home.** Turn off the cell phone and leave your CrackBerry in your bag at night and on weekends when you want quality time with your family. Just as when your boss or coworkers know they *can* contact you after hours, not being connected (and answering) will train them *not* to try unless absolutely necessary.

Change Your Job

It's a radical idea, I know, but think about the possibility that you can actually *change* your job rather than quit it. You can cut back hours by going to ten hours, four days a week. Factor in your commute time, cost of lunches, clothes, day care savings, physical and mental health, and quality of your life.

You can change your job by telecommuting one or two days, saving time, money, and brainpower. Working from home not only cuts the cost of fuel, tolls, and fares but also cuts the hours you spend commuting to and from your job. One or two days a week in your sweats will save on purchasing and maintaining work clothes. Women, think of the time you'll save by not doing the full makeup-and-hair thing. Men, shaving can be optional. With increased comfort and decreased interruptions, you'll find that you'll be more focused, creative, and productive.

With any change in an organization, don't approach your boss and say, "Can I telecommute/change hours?" The old saying "It's better to beg forgiveness than ask for permission" applies here. Craft your "forgiveness" by saying, "I've found that I can complete my paperwork more accurately and on time when I work uninterrupted at home. I'll be working from home on Wednesday for the next four weeks. If you are unhappy with my work, I'll go back to my regular schedule."

With any change, always

- ▶ Make an appointment for the request.
- ▶ Prepare your presentation with documentation or proof.
- ▶ Talk of benefits the company will get, not you.

Keeping Work at Work When You Work from Home

Working from home presents new challenges for separating your work and home life. Add to that working *with* your spouse or mate, and it could eliminate all your personal time if you're not vigilant. My neighbor and friend, Linda, is a highly successful artist who has her studio downstairs in her home. She creates beautiful paintings on silk, and her husband runs the business side of her art—she's the passionate, creative artist, and he's the pragmatic executive. This difference in outlook and separation of duties makes it difficult to keep business from invading their "us" time. She told me, "We need to be ruthless about keeping the business separate. We have friends over for fun, and we take trips where we can get away from it all, but we mostly need to guard against the little things like business discussions during dinner or thoughts that come into our head as we're dozing off to sleep: 'Did you remember to . . . ?' or 'Remind me tomorrow that we need to call . . .' " Keep in mind:

▶ **Set and stick to regular hours for working.** This enables your mind (and body) to switch gears to being present to where you are—either work or home.

▶ **Develop a way to "close" your home office.** Shut the door, put up a screen, throw a tablecloth over it, hang a "gone fishing" sign on the computer screen. It's the old adage: out of sight, out of mind.

▶ **Leave a mess occasionally.** You don't need to clean your desk for privacy or for appearances' sake. When you're working on a large, complex project and it's quitting time, leave all the papers and files in place with a sticky note where you can pick up where you left off.

▶ **Don't check e-mail after 6 P.M. or before your "opening time."** It will help you stick to your "office hours" and prevent "just one quick check" from consuming your evening with a response.

▶ **Turn off your electronics when it's family or me time.** That call, text, or e-mail alert is rarely convenient and always diminishes quality time.

▶ **Have a "switch gears" routine.** Do a sequence of activities in your home workspace that marks changing gears from home to work. Just a simple, easy system: open door; adjust lighting, music, and ventilation; get fresh glass of water; take a few deep breaths; perform a few light stretches; invoke a higher power; and smile.

Your Work Is Not Your Worth

How often have you gotten yourself so worked up at work because you've confused *what* you do with *who* you are? This happens when you're pushing the limits of your job—taking on more assignments, landing the big account, getting the promotion, banking the bonus—and you just seem to eat, sleep, and breathe your career. You can't seem to switch it off, because work is all you do. But no job or promotion can define your worth. You define your worth. Remember:

▶ **You are not what you do.** You are the sum total of your thoughts, beliefs, experience, commitments, and actions.

▶ **Don't be a walking résumé.** Get over yourself. Let your current actions and how you treat others speak louder than what you've accomplished.

▶ **Don't qualify yourself by talking about your job.** People will like and respect you more when you're *interested in* them, than *interesting to* them.

Make the Right Choice When It Comes to Work and Family

When navigating your business, keep the rest of your life alive and diverse. Remember your priorities away from work. Don't get confused about whether to attend a business development meeting or your child's Christmas play. Choose the family—make the choice that nourishes your home life and increases those moments that make life full and priceless.

You could get mad if the company makes you choose between them and your family. Instead, say, "I won't be at the meeting. I'll be at my daughter's holiday play/son's game/wife's recital. My family is the reason I can be my best when I'm working. Their love and support keep me going, and I don't want to miss these moments in their lives." Knowing what your priorities are in this regard will help you to change your attitude, curb your temper, and reduce stress.

Unwind and Recreate

The absolute best way to ensure that your personal life and your work life are separate, distinct entities is by making your home a place that you look forward to getting to when the day is done. By doing so, you will have a constant reminder of why you are going into work each day and a refuge away from the office as well. Your home needs to be relaxing and restoring to your soul. That doesn't mean plopping down in front of the computer or television. It means to break your rhythm and restructure your time, like spending quality time with the family or pursuing hobbies or leisure activities.

- ▶ **Make sure your days off are really *off*!** Do something besides errands, laundry, or catching up on work. Believe it or not, you won't get into the corner office by eating, breathing, and sleeping your job 24/7/365. You need a life. Take it back.
- ▶ **Plan a vacation.** The research and planning of any trip is a big part of the fun. Even if you don't know how you'll pay for it or who will take care of the cat and dog, often the universe will offer you ways. Your *intention* to take a trip will fire you up and make every brown bag lunch and late night project worth the effort. You may find yourself resisting extraneous expenditures,

researching new subjects, even learning a new language when you have a "grand adventure" on the planning boards.

▶ **Have a short "staycation."** Did you have campouts in the backyard as a kid? There was something adventurous about being away from home but having the comfort of knowing that you could run inside when the neighbor's cat tipped over a trash can. Plan your staycation as you would an out-of-town vacation. Get everyone involved, get guidebooks for your area, set a budget, pay the bills, and do house chores before you begin. Plan your days' events and activities, turn off all your electronics, change your outgoing message, and don't be tempted to do anything around the house. You'll be surprised at the fun you'll have eating out at breakfast, playing tennis on a public court, visiting local attractions, or taking a historical tour of your own town. Travel is great, but Old Faithful will be there next year.

▶ **Get a house project.** When we met, one of the strongest mutual attractions my husband and I had was our love of home improvement. He was impressed that I had my own set of power tools, and I loved that he could figure out how to fix *anything* and is very organized and tidy when he does so. Our happiest times together are when we are planning, shopping, building, or remodeling. I'm not suggesting everyone start tearing out walls. There are other projects that don't involve power tools, such as making memory books, researching the family tree, or painting a room.

▶ **Take up a new hobby.** Nothing is as humbling as tumbling down the bunny hill when you're first learning to ski or snowboard. And nothing as exhilarating! You're never too old to learn to pack your own chute, strap on a scuba tank, or collect baseball cards. With a new hobby or sport comes a new set of skills, people, and language. Immerse yourself and let the joy take you away.

A Healthy Balance Requires You to Be Healthy

There's a saying in the equestrian world: no hoof, no horse. The hoof is vitally important to the horse since it bears a huge proportion of the total weight and it indicates the soundness of the animal. For office-dwelling humans, your health bears a large proportion of balancing your life: no health, no soundness.

Increase Your Fuel Octane

If you're like most busy people, your diet is full of holes. Skipped meals, fast food, and liquid meals are those I hear about (and have experienced) the most. We all know we should eat better, but who has the time, inclination, and willpower? So we tend to swallow the latest vitamin and mineral pill to make up for our nutritional shortfall. Unfortunately, these pills and potions are expensive and are poor substitutes for a healthful diet, not to mention some can actually be harmful.

When it comes to diet and nutrition, my favorite voice of reason is Dr. Dean Edell and his book *Eat, Drink & Be Merry*. Dr. Edell believes that we should use common sense and a critical eye to make our personal health decisions. He warns us to be extremely mindful to distinguish between science and news. Science is proven through scientific method, which prevents research outcomes from being influenced by either the placebo effect or observer bias. News is trying to sell you something through anecdotal evidence—so-and-so says it worked, without any actual scientific proof.

Allow me to inject some sanity into your plan to eat better.

▶ **Give up on fad diets.** These usually promise quick results and deliver, but do you really want to live carb-free (or gluten-free or sodium-free) for the rest of your life? If you must diet, do it with tried-and-true methods such as Weight Watchers, which emphasize healthy weight loss along with information, support, simplicity, and accountability.

▶ **Eat a sensible diet** rich in fruits and vegetables, whole grains, and low-fat dairy products plus modest amounts of fish and low-fat meat and chicken.

▶ **If you need help, consult a *registered dietician* (R.D.).** A "nutritionist" is usually trying to sell you something, and it's *not* science.

▶ **Make a weekly meal plan (including snacks) and shop regularly.** If it isn't in the house, you can't make or eat it.

▶ **Carry food or brown bag it frequently.** You don't need to have a whole meal with you, just healthier snacks.

Get It Done Cookies. Ever since I discovered cookies and books at the foot of my crib on Saturday mornings, I've loved cookies (and books). It was my mother's way to keep me occupied so she and Dad could sleep in just a bit. Keeping with this "tradition," I still want to read and eat cookies first thing every morning. I've modified this recipe over the years, and I want to share it. The name came from being able to check off "breakfast," "fiber," and "snack" from my shopping and to-do list, plus the cookies' "regularity-inducing" properties.

Cream together:

¾ cup cholesterol-smart buttery spread
1 cup brown sugar
½ cup white sugar

Add in:

½ cup egg substitute
1 tablespoon vanilla

Mix separately, then add to above mixture:

¼ cup whole wheat flour
1 teaspoon pumpkin pie spice
1 teaspoon baking powder
¼ teaspoon baking soda

Mix in:

2 cups oat bran
2½ cups oats
1 cup puffed rice cereal
1 cup golden raisins (I don't like the dark ones.)
½ cup nuts (optional)
½ cup chocolate chips (optional)

Drop by cookie scoop (generous tablespoonful) onto nonstick cookie pan and bake at 375° in oven for 13 to 14 minutes. Cool and store in tight container.

Treat Your Body Right

Crazy busy can drastically affect your balance. Consider this scenario: Your big project makes you too busy to cook, so you eat in restaurants and grab fast food. You don't have time to exercise, so you gain a few extra pounds. The knees start to hurt, so you hire someone to walk your dog. You mask the pain with something over-the-counter and gain more weight. Your bowels rebel with diarrhea, your electrolytes get unbalanced, and your natural immunity is lowered. You catch the nasty cold that's going around, and your doctor can't see you for two days. As you nurse your fatigue, fever, and hacking cough, you miss a critical deadline and jeopardize a big project.

After years of working with sick people as a nurse and having had my share of health challenges, I know that if you don't have a healthy, pain-free body, nothing else really matters in life. While working in intensive care, I adjusted the morphine pumps of cancer patients and pumped the chests of heart attack victims. It's true, they would have given everything they had to be healthy. Our bodies change over time, but this doesn't necessarily have to be for the worse. Even though our health-care system is flawed (geared to *fixing*, rather than *preventing*, poor health), you can ensure your future wellness. Here are some important tips to help you do just that:

▶ **Find a doctor you can talk to, ask questions, and e-mail.** If money is an issue, don't discount your local free community clinic, because many fine health-care providers volunteer their services to these facilities.

▶ **Get a baseline checkup with blood work and urinalysis.** Many serious conditions and diseases show up here *way* before you get symptoms.

▶ **Use sunscreen and have a skin check.** A dermatologist can perform a "mole patrol" to catch cancer early and help you sidestep premature wrinkles.

▶ **Get your eyes checked.** Besides enabling you to see better, your eye doctor might identify why you have those blinding headaches or spot a problem before it affects your vision.

▶ **See a dentist.** Along with fixing cavities that release bacteria responsible for heart, lung, and gastrointestinal (GI) damage, regular visits to the dentist help you *keep* your teeth longer, improve (or brighten) your smile, and freshen your breath.

▶ **Learn to use a blood pressure machine.** Your blood pressure is not only a clear indication of your heart's function but of your overall health. Numbers don't lie; knowing your range and checking your blood pressure yourself allows you to "hear" what your heart may be telling you.

▶ **Stop smoking.** You'll save money and future problems (and people will like you better because you don't stink up their world).

▶ **Take a walk break** at work to clear your head and straighten your desk-bound posture.

▶ **Practice "safe office."** Wash your hands, use tissues for coughs and sneezes, and clean your phone, keyboard, mouse, and other well-used items.

▶ **Plan vacation time and scheduled breaks from the office.**

Get Sexy, Smart, and Slim Through Sleep

Are you tired of being tired? When you're busy, something's got to give, and it's usually your sleep. It starts innocently— a half an hour here, a late night there—then you're up half the night with a sick child or worried about a big presentation. The next day you're powering down the energy drinks to make it through the afternoon, and when you finally get home and hit the sack, you can't fall or stay asleep.

It's no secret that a busy lifestyle can affect your sleep habits, and the proof is in the numbers. The National Sleep Foundation reports that more than twenty million women are tossing and turning every night. Here are more facts from surveys of the sleepless.

▶ 60 percent of women get a good night's sleep only a couple of times a week.
▶ 72 percent of stay-at-home moms, 72 percent of working moms, and 68 percent of single working women don't get enough sleep or have problems falling or staying asleep.
▶ 100 percent of sleep-deprived women just suck it up and go on, 80 percent of them report that they never get a chance to catch up.
▶ 67 percent of the sleep deprived use caffeine to keep them alert during the day.
▶ 33 percent of sleep-deprived women have given up sex.
▶ And, according to the National Highway Safety Administration, 37 percent of sleep-deprived women have fallen asleep at the wheel.

Yikes! It's frightening to think that there are so many out there going through the day without enough sleep to function properly. These people are practically ticking time bombs waiting to go off! If you are among the league of zombies, it is time for you to adjust the way you sleep. Here are some tips to increase your sleep quantity and quality:

▶ Have a wind-down routine that begins at the same time each night and ends with you going to bed.
▶ Don't go to sleep while watching TV. Researchers at Stanford University found that the light from your monitor can reset your wake/sleep cycle by hours.
▶ Take a class on guided imagery or relaxation.
▶ Use products containing lavender or chamomile or find some bedtime music with a tempo of sixty to eighty beats per minute.

▶ Lower the temperature of your bedroom, take a hot bath, and turn off night-lights, including clock radio and phone lights.

▶ Wearing socks warms your feet and legs, allowing your internal body temperature to drop, signaling to your body it's time for sleep.

▶ Use spongy earplugs to block out distractions.

▶ Block your bedmate's snoring. Discuss with your partner how his or her snoring keeps you up and affects the quality and quantity of your sleep. Together, explore treatments and ways to prevent it. If it's the dog, put Fido in another room.

▶ Put the kids to bed earlier. They need more sleep, and you can reconnect with your partner.

▶ Have sex. Studies at the Kettering Medical Center in Ohio found the big O a fast-acting, healthy alternative to medication.

Being the granddaughter of mattress makers, I'd be remiss if I didn't encourage you to get a good mattress along with the right pillow, comfy linens, and natural blankets. Always on the lookout for a way to improve our sleep, my husband and I bought one of those "space-age" mattresses that mold to your body. The first night, after reading for our standard fifteen minutes, we leaned over for a good-night kiss before we turned out the lights only to discover we were *stuck* in what felt like warm bread dough! We replaced the mattress even though it gave us a good laugh. (And who couldn't use more giggles in bed?)

Get Happy with You

While it's important to eat well and work out, what is even more important is to make peace with your body—be happy with what you've got. This one act can save your health and your money. When you're not trying to look like an air-brushed, photoshopped celebrity, you'll start to treat yourself better.

▶ Change your ideals and find some new heroes or heroines.
▶ Minimize reading fashion magazines. Those aren't *real* women or men, only handpicked human coat hangers barely out of their teens.
▶ Don't watch makeover television shows. Plastic surgery doesn't always solve self-image problems, and it should not be held up as the ideal solution to physical imperfection.
▶ Get a uniform that's "you." Wear clothes that you look great in, toss your fat wardrobe, and forget the skinny jeans.
▶ Get a hairstyle that allows you to "fix it and forget it."
▶ Love that you're forty (or fifty, sixty, seventy). You earned it!

The Other People in Your Life

It's true that no man (or woman) is an island. I agree with Margaret Mead's statement that "One of the oldest human needs is having someone to wonder where you are when you don't come home at night." And I don't believe that just any old "someone" will do. When it comes to balancing your life, your friends and lovers are either contributing to it or contaminating it. Therefore, it's time to really scrutinize those folks you allow in your life.

Stop Looking for Love (Let It Find You)

My first book, *Finding Love (Again!)*, was focused on dating and finding the right partner. After being widowed at twenty-six, I spent twenty years (and sixteen days and five hours) dating and researching dating skills before I married my husband. I know what works and doesn't work. One thing I know for sure is that looking for the right person for the right reasons and doing it right is like having an extra job. And in order to meet the right person, *you must first be the right person.*

I have personally coached dozens of men and women to find love and have given seminars on dating to thousands. I've heard so many stories and challenges, heartbreaks and breakups from both sexes that I rarely get surprised anymore. It takes energy, time, and money to look for love. Many times I have shocked someone by telling him or her to not date or even think about looking for love! My best advice I give you here:

▶ **Go on a dating fast and don't date *anyone.*** This is especially necessary if you've just gotten out of a bad relationship or have been dating a lot of "junk food" (dating bad people or those who just got out of a bad relationship). Your heart and mind need a break in order to tune in to what you really want and need in a companion.

▶ **Stop worrying about finding "the one."** It dilutes your energy and focus for a balanced life, and you'll be putting out a desperate vibe that drives love *away* from you.

▶ **Stop listening to your biological clock ticking.** Fulfill your nurturing needs by taking care of the child inside of you.

▶ **Stop looking, scheming, and thinking you *need* a partner.** Maybe the path of your purpose is to be single right now.

▶ **Become the kind of person with whom you want to spend the rest of your life.** How can you attract and keep Mr. or Ms. Right if you're all wrong? Practice kindness, clean up your credit, keep your promises, save some money, honor your commitments, make your house a home.

▶ **Use your dating fast as impetus to de-busify your life quicker.** Hormones and the urge to mate is the strongest force you've got in your arsenal against your crazy-busy lifestyle.

▶ **If you're married (estranged or separated), learn to love the mate you have better, stronger, deeper.** The grass is usually *not* greener, so consider personal help or couples' counseling.

Many years ago, I attended a financial conference that offered a panel of millionaires giving tips for becoming rich. All of them agreed that marrying the right person directly influences your millionaire status. They didn't mean to marry a high earner or someone with a large inheritance. Rather, they concurred that a person with your same values and goals will enable you to *stay* married, thusly avoiding divorce. Therefore, I say, *choose wisely.*

Go on a Favor Diet

Another way you can add balance to your life with regard to other people is to cut down on doing the favors they ask of you. You know the friends and family members who ask ever so nicely, "Could you pleeease do this one little favor for me?" You know when it's not really little and when it's a demand instead of a favor. And at times they get mad at you because you don't acquiesce. Doing some favors here and there is the mark of a good friend or relative, but there's a fine line between being a good friend and being a doormat. Eventually too many of these little favors can add up if you're not careful and take up a wide chunk of your schedule. If you feel yourself being oppressed by too many favors, just say no.

Here are the keys to refusing those people you don't work with who ask too many favors and aren't gracious when you refuse:

- ▶ **Don't explain why you can't.** "Gosh, no, I can't do that for you."
- ▶ **Don't apologize.** "No, that's family day around here."
- ▶ **Don't buy into their anger or snit.** Their game only works if you buy into it.
- ▶ **Do be pleasant.** You're contributing to a kinder, gentler society.
- ▶ **Do stick to your refusal.** They'll stop asking you when they learn they can't convince or guilt you into acquiescing.
- ▶ **Do let it go.** Shrug your shoulders, forget it, and get on with your life.

Some Friends Need to Grow Away

Spending less time with friends with whom you don't have great relationships with frees up time in your life to help you to get your "busy" under control. Maybe they're stuck in the past, and you've moved on mentally, spiritually, and relationally. Often this occurs when the relationship's pain outweighs the gain and you must face a hard truth: Would I be better off with or without this person in my life? There are many reasons why you should let a friendship go. Do you let it die a natural death by ignoring it or formally end it by having a final discussion? Yes, no, maybe, it depends.

This isn't something to take lightly, though. If and when you do decide to end a friendship, you must keep your own counsel about it. It's important that you don't try to get a consensus from other friends. Instead, if you must talk to someone, talk to a professional or an impartial third party.

I have tried to break up gracefully with my friends whenever the need has arisen, but it is emotionally extremely difficult. Believe me, I've botched it as many times as not. But after the final good-bye and I'm relieved of the toxicity from the relationship, I wondered why I didn't do it sooner. And, yes, friends have dismissed me, as well. Did I ever find out why? Sometimes. Did it hurt? Yes, but the gain of my peace outweighed the pain of peace between us.

Your Master Plan

Finding your authentic self is a powerful way to get balance back in your life. Most of us are so busy running around putting out fires that we don't have time to get perspective on our life and goals. It starts with creating a master plan for your life that includes identifying your goals in the six areas of your life from your satisfaction wheel in Chapter 1. This is the beginning of a process that ends with you running your own life instead of it running you.

In a spiral-bound notebook, write each of the following six headings at the top of a page. Leave yourself room to write under the heading and halfway down each page write, "What I need to be, do, or have to accomplish this."

▶ **Business and career.** What do you want your life's work to be or look like? How many hours a week? What location? What do you want your legacy to be?
▶ **Financial and investment.** How much money and savings do you need? How can you get that? What can you let go of?

▶ **Physical and appearance.** Your health is a pivotal point in balancing your life. How are you going to achieve this? What do you need?

▶ **Self-development and recreation.** How are you of service to the greater world? How can you recreate *you* in your balanced vision?

▶ **Relationships with people.** What does your chosen family look like? Who do you need to release, forgive? What rituals can you institute to be balanced?

▶ **Home and environment.** Is your home a sanctuary? What do you need to make the world around you more loving and beautiful?

Let this be a multipage essay you work on for the next two weeks. It is harder than you think to identify your deepest hopes, wishes, and dreams. Beware that this process takes time and honesty. Many of my students use my "imbalance detox" method to complete this exercise.

Imbalance Detox

For the next two weeks when you're at home, limit your Internet activity to fifteen minutes a day, have no personal chats on the phone, watch no television, turn off the radio, don't read any magazines or newspapers, prepare and eat simple meals, do minimal laundry and housekeeping, shop only for groceries, attend no social activities, and accept no outside business engagements. On your outgoing voice mail, say, "I'm on a new project, please contact me on _____ (date two weeks hence)."

Once you've articulated your big picture, you can break each major goal into yearly goals and tasks. From your yearly goals, you will have your monthly and weekly goals to achieve the kind of balance you want. Of course, all along this process you need to constantly challenge your goals.

- ▶ Is this what I really want?
- ▶ Should I *let go of* this person, place, or thing?
- ▶ Will this get me more in balance?
- ▶ Is this SMART?

Chart a SMART Course

With the advent of global positioning systems in our computers, cars, and wristbands, it's nearly impossible to get lost. Satellites can pinpoint where you are on earth by as close as a few feet. So far, though, they can't tell you where to go unless you program your destination. That is exactly how your life works: you'll get lost a lot less on your road to balance if you know your destination.

When earning my private pilot's license, I learned the dire importance of *planning*. To get to the fun part (flying to a destination), there was a lot of time spent on the ground. I also spent many hours in the air practicing bank turns over the ocean or shooting "touch-and-gos" (landing and immediately taking off again). The importance of filing a flight plan for any trip was drummed into me. It forced me to plan my trip to insure safely arriving at my destination.

In filing a flight plan, I needed to state my departure point and time, type and ID of my aircraft, special equipment on board, the proposed route, cruising altitude, airspeed, checkpoints, as well as estimated time en route, destination, fuel on board, and pilot information. Is it any wonder I love flying, with all the details? All this planning and study made me feel smart.

When you plan the flight that is your life, choose a SMART course.

S Make your goals **specific**. "Get healthy" is not specific, but "I will lose fifteen pounds and keep my cholesterol level below 200" is clear and well defined. Be really specific with your goals—you might just get what you hope for.

M Your goals should be **measurable**. Old joke: How do you eat an elephant? One bite at a time. To make a goal measurable, make it quantifiable by breaking it into smaller, more manageable tasks. Each step sequentially leads to the next, and you know exactly how far along you are.

A Your goals should be **attuned** to your life as a whole. Is your goal compatible with your overall plan? Most sales organizations have quotas along with contests and awards for the top producers. I spent eleven years in such a company and found selling to be rewarding but all-consuming. Each quarterly meeting I found my competitive juices flowing as I'd vow to be in the top producers club. When I finally made it to the top, I realized that it was just not possible to work so many hours (350 days a year!) if I wanted any kind of balanced life.

R Your goals should be **realistic**. They say overnight success usually takes about seventeen years. Don't go hoping that it's all going to happen overnight for you. Be realistic about what you want to accomplish and also how long you think it will take.

T Have a **timetable** attached to your goals. When you assign a timetable to your goal, you eliminate the feeling that you're living your life with one foot nailed to the floor, going in circles. As with measurability, you'll gain patience and perspective knowing you're heading in the right direction.

Launch Your Balanced Life

Ever since I took my first flight lesson, I wanted to fly a blimp, so I put it on my goal list. I was told this would be impossible, doors were slammed in my face, and people laughed at me as they hung up. As I said, some things are difficult, and the impossible just takes a little more time and planning.

Years later I was climbing aboard the Goodyear blimp as a passenger while the ground crew readied to launch the 192-foot long, 60-foot high airship. Upon the pilot's command, twenty-two burly guys held onto lines to float the airship a foot above the ground. They started a slow, rhythmic chant, "One-ah. Two-ah. Three-ah. Good!" Soon they began pulling us forward, bouncing and chanting, "One-ah. Two-ah. Three-ah. Good!" Just about the time I thought we were gaining elevation, we *slammed* into the ground on the word "good." Sandbags were pulled out of compartments, and we floated up six feet. We continued bouncing forward, "One-ah. Two-ah. Three-ah. Good!" With each cycle, more sandbags were removed. One final "good!" *slam*, and the crew let go of the lines. Oh, the thrill! Once airborne, I asked the pilot, "Can I fly it?" He got out of his seat and said, "She's all yours."

It was a wonderful experience, but more important, I learned something I'd like to pass on to you: Life is like taking off in a blimp. You'll think it's difficult—and sometimes impossible—but if you make your plan, keep moving forward with the help of your crew, bounce up when you're slammed to the ground, and let go of what's weighing you down, *you will fly* and never find yourself too busy for your own good.

Conclusion

Raiders of the Lost Spark

We know what we are, but know not what we may be.

—William Shakespeare

Humanity evolved into what it is today because the good women and men outnumbered the bad ones. People like yourself who concentrate on doing good, being strong in the face of adversity, and staying committed to learning. For every person who stands in the way of getting your "busy" under control, there are four or five willing to help you. This has got to be true, or we would still be using stone tools and living in caves.

It used to be an accepted fact that the brain doesn't change much past a certain age. Now we know that your brain is constantly changing. Cognitive dissonance dictates that your brain is always changing to prove the reality of what you believe. Your brain can't hold conflicting ideas without making you uncomfortable enough to question the inconsistencies of your behaviors.

If you're dissatisfied with your overbusy lifestyle but you hold the belief that it will make you happy and fulfilled, your brain senses a conflict or an inconsistency. Your brain uses this inconsistency to motivate you to change. Don't stick with your old thoughts, beliefs, and actions with regard to your day-to-day life. Life can be what you want it to be. Having a new outlook will change your crazy-busy lifestyle into one that has meaning and purpose. You will recapture your lost spark and bring back balance into your life.

You Must Be PRESENT to Win

Have you ever entered a contest for something you really wanted, such as a vacation or new car? Somewhere on the drawing card is the phrase *You must be present to win*. If you really want to balance your life, you must be PRESENT to win it:

P **Prioritize** what's important for your **purpose**.

R **Rest** and **restore** your body.

E **Eliminate** clutter and **enjoy** what you have.

S **Set** goals that are **SMART**.

E **Encourage** harmonious relationships.

N Say **no** more often.

T **Trust** in something greater than yourself.

This Is Your Do-Over

It is rough out here in the real world. You lose loved ones, your kids get into trouble, people lie, cheat, and steal from you, and superiors demand that you march to the beat of their drum. Our overbusy, continuously connected society has actually separated us from our true passions. You may say, "I know I should take control of my busyness, but I don't have the time right now, and my finances are a mess." You might even fear that people would be angry with you or you'd lose ground and end up with nothing. But it doesn't have to be that way. You don't have to continue the too-busy lifestyle that you've been practicing. You have a chance for a do-over when you summon up the courage to stand up for what is best for you.

The truth is that it's not lack of time or money that's holding you back. The main reason you don't cut out all your busyness is one thing: a lack of belief—you lack belief that your life will actually be better if you do what needs to be done to get it there. You've got to *believe* things can be better for you. You've got to believe that miracles can happen for you. Otherwise, they most definitely will not be happening for you.

There's Only One You

Like you, Ludwig van Beethoven lived a life surrounded by many people who wanted a piece of him. As with many great artists of the time, he had a patron, a prince who supported him while he composed. Like you, he had times when it was demanded he abandon his principles in order to fulfill some obligation.

At one time in their relationship, Beethoven's patron demanded he dedicate a symphony to Napoleon in order to gain the general's favor. They were in the patron's castle just outside of Vienna, where Napoleon's soldiers were billeted. When Beethoven found out what a tyrant Napoleon was, he refused to dedicate the symphony out of principle for his art. He sent his patron a note: "What you are, you are by accident of birth; what I am, I am by myself. There are and always will be thousands of princes, but there is only one Beethoven." This is the very man who asked before his death, "I did have a certain amount of talent, didn't I?"

In all of us, there are two people—the believer and the cynic. The believer says, "Yes I can! There is only one me!" Your cynic says, "Oh, I don't think anything is ever going to change. I'm just another cog in the machine."

Stop! Celebrate the believer in you who wants peace, joy, strength, and love. Let go! Let the world know that there is only one *you.*

Dear Reader,

You and your experiences, tips, and stories are an ongoing interest to me. If we have the pleasure of meeting in person, I look forward to hearing your thoughts and comments. You can also contact me online by visiting my websites at TooBusyforYourOwnGood.com and TooBusyNo More.com; please be sure to join my community when you do.

Index